Collected Poems

Born in 1932, the son of a Dublin bricklayer, Christy Brown was the victim of the athenoid variety of cerebral palsy. With the help of his family and Dr Robert Collis, he overcame his physical disability and won immediate fame with his bestselling novel about life in Dublin, DOWN ALL THE DAYS. His other novels are MY LEFT FOOT, A SHADOW IN SUMMER, A PROMISING CAREER and WILD GROW THE LILIES. He died in 1981.

To Chrissie
lots of love
Irene
"Happy Reading"
1990. ☺

*Also by Christy Brown
and available in Minerva*

My Left Foot
Down all the Days
A Shadow on Summer
Wild Grow the Lilies
A Promising Career

CHRISTY BROWN

Collected Poems

Minerva

A Minerva Paperback

COLLECTED POEMS

First published in Great Britain as
Come Softly to My Wake (1971)
Background Music (1973)
Of Snails and Skylarks (1977)
by Martin Secker & Warburg Limited

This edition first published 1982

This Minerva edition published 1990
by Mandarin Paperbacks
Michelin House, 81 Fulham Road, London SW3 6RB

Minerva is an imprint of the Octopus Publishing Group

Copyright © 1971, 1973, 1977, 1982 by Christy Brown
Introduction copyright © Frank Delaney 1982

A CIP catalogue record for this title
is available from the British Library
ISBN 0 7493 9178 2

Printed and bound in Great Britain
by Cox and Wyman Ltd, Reading, Berks

Contents

Introduction   ix

COME SOFTLY TO MY WAKE

Come Softly to My Wake   3
Fog   4
Wishful   6
What Her Absence Means   7
Routine   9
Idyll   10
Poem to Margaret   11
Amour Profane   12
One Day and Another   14
Lines of Leaving   16
The Hooley   17
Windy Interlude   19
Surf   20
Sunday Morning   21
High Noon   22
In Passing   23
Lines out of Nowhere   24
Abel   25
Meridian   26
Multum in Parvo   27
Inheritance   28
Frostbite   30
Spring   31
My Ship   32
Muted   33
Waking   35
The Lost Prize   36
Eureka Etcetera   38
City Cameo   40
Possession   41

End 42
Revisited 43
Brendan 45
A Kind of Lament for Patrick Kavanagh 47
To Helen Keller 49
For My Mother 51
A Better than Death Wish 53

BACKGROUND MUSIC

Towards Morning 57
Drinking Song 58
City Dweller 60
Distance 61
Fallen Masonry 62
Good Friday 63
Her Absence 64
Finding 66
In Retrospect 67
In the Theatre Box 68
Invocation 69
Last Post 70
Lines for Lioba 72
Lines of Leaving 74
Looking at a Photograph 75
Lucy 76
Meeting 78
Poem for Sean Collis 79
The Drink 81
Mutability 83
My Brothers 84
My Credo As Of Now 85
My Mother's Son 86
Nemesis 88
Poem on a Monday Morning 90
Rainbow in Exeter 92
Sunday Sequence 94
Sunday Visit 97
The History Teacher 99

The Night Before The Morning After 100
The Visit 102
The Wait 103
Windy Interlude 104
Wishful 105
Young Charm 106
Anne 107
At Caragh House 108
At Closing Time 109
A Dirge Yet Not A Dirge 111
A Lesson Unlearned 114
After-Meeting 116
How to be Bored in Paradise 118
Honeymoon 119
For Prince 120
On the Beach 121
Sitting 122

OF SNAILS AND SKYLARKS

Sunset Star 125
Finding 126
W. H. Auden 128
Love Song 130
City Airs 131
Act of Contrition 132
Of Snails and Skylarks 134
Now and Not Then 136
In Memory of Melba Our Cat 137
Pique 138
The Poetry Reading 140
Victoria 142
Vamp 144
Lonely Madrigal 146
Over The Sea To Leeds 148
Broken Rhythm 149
Terminal Thoughts 150
Lapwing 152
A Kind of Prayer 153

John Millington Synge 155
Lost Item 156
Cobra 158
Morning Glory 160
Dear Dilemma 161
Dolphins 163
A Song For My Body 164
Memo to a Fellow Sufferer 167
Nocturnal 168
The Dunce 169
Moon Rise 171
Remembering A Friend: Robert Collis 173
Men At Work 175
A Handful of Haiku 176
Back At Base 178
Unearned Income 180
Beloved Myth 182
Past Portrait 184
Morning Song 185
Constancy 186
Sour Note On A Sweet Ending 188
A Blunt Instrument 190
Billy Nowhere 191
Lost Lullaby 193
Oriental 194
Slug Song 196
A Question For Myself 198
In Absentia 199
Visitors 201
Old Lady 202
Harlequinade 203

Introduction
by Frank Delaney

Choose a matrix from which writers are ideally fashioned and you meet the word "Ireland". An island – melancholy on the end of Europe; colourful – purpled and softened by the mountains and the rain; a race apart – oppressed by England, religion and a petty bourgeoisie, in that order. Above all, though, the Irish are outsiders. Never mind the bonhomie, the personable, tip-o'-the-wink, top-o'-the-morning, tipstering, toping skin. Beneath lies calm, cold even, often classical observation, plus a permanent desire for disengagement – all gifts to writers.

And they have displayed the gifts. James Joyce fled deeper into his soul – deliberate exile in Italy, Switzerland, France, with, as his only weapons, "silence, exile and cunning". The poet William Butler Yeats died in France, lamenting the onset of the post-revolutionary "grocers' republic". Samuel Beckett still lives in Paris.

Is the more triumphant writer, though, the one who stays and still remains an outsider? Christy Brown, late and loved, was such. From birth he was exiled by cerebral palsy, which stifled his verbal articulation and in some gorgeous epiphany blessed with movement only his left foot. So, he sat among the world, protected by his disability, and his spirit was like a winepress which poured out – how he would have hooted at the metaphor – through his left foot!

There is a life beneath the life of Dublin, down below the mortgage payments, down below the dole queue, where survival begins. In Christy Brown's day, it was a brawling, pawn-shop existence, where wives wore cheap face-cream to hide the bruises of wedded bliss. When his novel *Down all the Days* was published in 1970, the torrent of words, necklaced from shock to shock, immediately established his stature as the observer of that life, as the outsider who sat among it, was not of it, shielded by the luck of his disability. He was, in his work, a painter in the style they call "primitive".

I remember the night he appeared on Ireland's principal television programme, *The Late Late Show*. He sat there like a little hunched, raddled troll, whose efforts to speak boomed at the audience. His wheelchair matched the chrome hardware of the television studio, and he had a grin on his face. Instantly it was apparent that here was a man who had the true writer's gifts. Not only was he an outsider – he had a huge secret, like a tramp with a tremendous fortune, or clerk who is a great lover. Christy Brown may have been crippled from birth, forced to accept help and compassion in order merely to stay alive, but he had his secret.

The secret – perhaps, finally, the greatest of a writer's gifts – did not appear willingly in his prose. But it did in his poems. Once, in a brief and crowded conversation, I told him the legend of the discovery of champagne. A French monk tasted the accidental output of the winepress and exclaimed: "But I am drinking the stars." Christy Brown rocked a little with delight and his eyes gleamed. Just at that moment he was the writer who unveils all his secrets in his poems, these poems, hereafter.

Come Softly to My Wake

Come Softly to My Wake

Come softly to my wake
on Pavlova feet
at the greying end of day;
into the smoke and heat
enter quietly smiling, quietly unknown
among the garrulous guests
gathered in porter nests
to reminisce and moan;
come not with ornate grief
to desecrate my sleep
but a calm togetherness of hands
quiet as windless sands
and if you must weep
be it for the old quick lust
now lost in dust
only you could shake
from its lair.

Come softly to my wake
and drink and break
the rugged crust
of friendly bread
and weep not for me dead
but lying stupidly there
upon the womanless bed
with a sexless stare
and no thought in my head.

Fog

A lugubrious foghorn in the shrouded distance
scarves of mist swirling up the avenue;
in the grey garden over the way
a red-hulled little boat stood perched
as out of depth as I.
Obscure glints of light in the goldfish bowl
the ancient Alsatian lolling at my feet
fleece technicoloured from the carpet dye.
Crunch of wheels on gravel.

I pensively sipped my drink
staring out at the unseen lawn
hearing her quiet movements in the kitchen
preparing lunch for her children
answering their unanswerable questions.

At last briefly alone
we discussed careful, unhurtful things.
The lithograph above the fireplace
surrealist symbol of a wedding feast
an obese satyr keeled over dead drunk
gnomic guests floating eerily in the shadows
hardly in life
hardly delineated.
She knelt to heap more coal on the fire
her face lit by the jealous flames
warmly in life
perfectly delineated.

The old tenderness breeding the old pain
creeping across the whispering room
not to be drowned on any amber sea of burnt brandy.
My trapped senses slid and slithered on ice
hot as the hissing coals.
I stared at a pair of her faded pink slippers
imagined her toes in them

most ordinary and naked
and savagely devoured my drink.

I did not understand the taximan's anger
taking me brutally back
under the haloed lights of the city.
For in all that furious fog
foaming and fuming in from the invisible sea
he had merely lost his way.

Wishful

I would be free of pavements
newspapers of no news
clocks that bully my existence
cars that whisk me away like God
descending unannounced upon me
buses that move as lugubrious elephants
horses fettered to the stupid hands of men.

I am tired to tears of the mental life
of my room full of the ghosts
of never-known things
this spluttering monster machine
creaking into rusty senility
its hammerstrokes deciphering for innocent posterity
my heart's sudden audaciousness.

I would gather about me soft-sandalled things
shadows on a burning lake
trees bending to the earth in love.
Where oh where are the beautiful people?
– the quick of wit
the clowns who spit
in life's sanctimonious countenance
the insolent
the indolent
the fey and gay
with sunlight dripping down their limbs?

I would pawn my hypothetical soul
to wake sudden in the dawn
and find a girl's footprints in dew outside my door.

What Her Absence Means

It means
    no madcap delight will intrude
into the calm flow of my working hours
    no ecstatic errors perplex
my literary pretensions.

It means
    there will be time enough for thought
undistracted by brown peril of eye
    and measured litany of routine deeds
undone by the ghost of a scent.

It means
    my neglect of the Sonnets will cease
and Homer come into battle once more.
    I might even find turgid old Tennyson
less of a dead loss now.

It means
    there will be whole days to spare
for things important to a man –
    like learning to live without a woman
without altogether losing one's mind.

It means
    there is no one now to read my latest poem
with veiled unhurried eyes
    putting my nerves on the feline rack
in silence sheer she-devil hell for me.

It means
    there is no silly woman to tell me
"Take it easy – life's long anyway –
don't drink too much – get plenty of sleep –"
    and other tremendous clichés.

It means
    I am less interrupted now with love.

Routine

There is a pattern in sinning
that takes the savour from the act.
Today I could weep for my sins
and tomorrow call myself a fool
yielding to the after-tiredness of indulgence.
There's no use crying over spilt sperm.
What I do and regret today
I'll do and regret tomorrow
and whatever other tomorrow I may see
with undiminished intensity.

Sin on a grand scale wouldn't be so bad.
Three-dimensional
Todd-AO
auditory, visual, aromatic, cinemascopic sin
with a beat and a boom and a bang to it.
Sin biblical as Saul struck blind
and Magdalen's breasts curving over the dawn.
It is the inch-by-wary-inch
antiseptic, deodorised, medically approved
behind-closed-shutters
closed-circuit, do-it-yourself type of sin-making
that sucks a man dry
as a well-sucked orange
trapping the poor wriggling eel-like thoughts
in the wet and ragged net
of his dull iniquities.

A glass of fine brandy renders some solace
and even at today's price
is cheaper than a full confession.

Idyll

Shall we go and lean by the river
in the dusk and peace under the old red bridge
where thoughts fall cool as leaves
beyond the barbed-wire fence of words?

Shall we go out from the city
    the little stone habitats of pin-striped people
    the twilight lovers of much knowledge and little faith;
    the tired time-killers, youth-killers, lady-killers
    making lugubrious love by electric clocks;
    the bottom-kissers of arid ambition,
    the soapbox demagogues of mangled moralities
    with their little household gods
    of security, swivel chairs, position, trim lawns, trim lusts,
    semi-detached conjugalities in suburbia,
    their weekend-away-from-home idyll,
    contraceptives secreted in pound-pregnant wallets
    in whose martini mouths love is a sniggered aside
    bandied about from bedroom to bedroom, bosom to bosom
    in dull debauchery of denuded sense . . .
Shall we go lest we become less than magnanimous
    and end by impossibly hating them?

Shall we go and lean by the river
in the dusk and peace under the old red bridge
where the water is clear as the mind never is
and the fishes do not wish to go to the moon?

Poem to Margaret

Child of light
skipping down the eggshell path
of your butterfly years

yellow tendrils
skying wild behind you
swept back by your delight

a flower about to open
about to gladden the world
petal by milky petal

gather me a daisy chain
made from your joy
to wear in my winter

when the glow of now
pales to the far scent
of fragile frost

Margaret of the marigold ways
running across deep October fields
drowning me in the pollen

of your madcap years
making pain seem solace
all child and sudden wisdom

amazing me.

Amour Profane

I shall watch you in the dawn
come slowly awake
slightly bemused by it all
your after-love face
terror gone
hunger slaked
a young girl again
naked and new
that night having lain
not merely with a lover
but love.

We will talk clear words
in the calm after love
catch new worlds
in the shape of each shadow.
Not for us the man-woman prison
of the normal and healthy
the normal and selfish
the slow gnawing of years
the slow bite of cancer
shredding bruised minds.
Scourge of routine
scourge of security
ceremony of love
without celebration
rounding our days to a covenant.
Love is not bound
save by freedom
and love's final word
remains unuttered.
Even we in our slight wisdom
know this.

I shall watch you in the dawn
tumble from sleep
the mist gone
and I content
with the knowledge of you on earth.

One Day and Another

Arrival

Within the desert of my arms
where you have never lain
I hold the yesterday shadow of you
subtle and gone as smoke.

Within my celibate cell
where late you sat bringing light
I hold your fragile fragrance
safe from the jealous wind.

Into my tomfoolery tumble of words
falling from me as blood
did your heart catch the whisper of a pain
too loud to be heard?

Within my hovel of flesh
you made brief haven of my loss
and I hold your shadow as hostage
past the last dying of my savage hope.

II
Non-Arrival

You did not come.
And as far as I know the world went on
spinning on its merry murderous way
and the clock chimed brutally on
and nothing very disastrous happened.
I even heard people go singing down the street
singing me out of existence.

The face upon my canvas today
is ugly and doomed as hope gone mad
and I envy it its final despair.

Poems run amok in my room
demented denizens of my livid hours
cruelly aborted out of this rage
stinging my senses – as burning flesh
burning at heart's-dead-end of day.

You did not come.
And the whiskey tastes remarkably the same—
my poison now as love was once.

Lines of Leaving

I am losing you again
all again
as if you were ever mine to lose.
The pain is as deep
beyond formal possession
beyond the fierce frivolity of tears.

Absurdly you came into my world
my time-wrecked world
a quiet laugh below the thunder.
Absurdly you leave it now
as always I foreknew you would.
I lived on an alien joy.

Your gentleness disarmed me
wine in my desert
peace across impassable seas
path of light in my jungle.

Now uncatchable as the wind you go
beyond the wind
and there is nothing in my world
save the straw of salvation in the amber dream.
The absurdity of that vast improbable joy.
The absurdity of you gone.

The Hooley

A quick hairtossing turn of head
    and down the narrow aisle of tables you came
        to where I sat a bitter, convivial host
           in a cage of chattering guestbirds
under a sham painting of an absurd youth
    poised girlishly in midstream beneath the Argus bell
        that the happily unenlightened call capital Art.
An hour since I had watched for you
    out into the early streetlamp-lit dusk,
        sternly undrunk in pressed suit and tie
           despite that day's dull debaucheries,
and fumed at your latecoming as at a slowcoach wife;
    left the house in fine fettle of anger,
        and so sat in a corner of crowded desolation
           till with swift hairtossing turn of head
you came, spying me instantly out in the sweat and smoke
        and sat beside me not saying much.
The spray of outflung words fell about me uncaught;
    briefly I sailed out from your haven
        on a porpoise wave of alcohol
           to some fragile shore of peace
a Crusoe in tortured quest of Girl Friday,
    seeking you beyond the bruised moment,
        the breakneck pace of the galloping hours;
           and found only silence huge and coiled
prowling in the undergrowth of panic
    drowning me in its enraged sealion's roar.

Somewhere on the humpbacked midnight
    in the jampacked, sardine-tight, rollicking house
        I found you in the coolness of the window –
           islanded on the sealapping fringe
of faces, voices, feet din-drumming
    and your eyes were murderously gentle
        in their brown seafoam gaze
           as I mouthed my bullying, prison cell love

and soft without intent
  I touched your near, bare arm
   in dumbplay of deafmute need
from out the harpooned heart of that hour,
    and fell back defeated by love,
and sailed far out upon the dim seas of my loss
  though I cried to you passionately
    all along the dead-shore of that dead, dead sea;
somewhere in the depths of that jezebel-ridden night
  of bronzed, brazen bewildered uproar I lost you,
    and I did not even know.

Windy Interlude

On that ribbon road in the hills
you wool-jacketed against the wind
above the river and the rock-leaping children
we dissected the bones of old hurts
laughed gravely at old fallacies
told ourselves brave unhappy things
in sudden break-away audacity of heart
I seeing not the uncertain sky
but the ever-changing heaven of your face
my heart glutted on this wonder
you most near
the green freedom around us
the tumult in the peace of that day.

The first slow raindrop touched my cheek;
I did not heed it
peacock-proud by you
this moment never to be betrayed
on this leaden earth.
Your head was bare
leaving your hair to blow in the wind.
Upon your sudden-remote face
a tremendous understanding
as if you knew why the day had turned traitor
and the curlew's cry died even as we heard it.

You did not see me then.
Something deeper held your eye and heart
and made the impetuous word die upon my tongue.

Surf

The wind swept along the deserted promenade
Tossing the screeching gulls aloft
as hieroglyphics in the wet smoking air.
Out towards Howth the lighthouse stood
shrouded in the lonely mist. I was glad
nobody was there this scene to share.
The day was brother to my mood.
Then sudden below the parapet in the soft
dull sand lay a girl in a red raincoat
and a thin-templed man with sloping shoulders.
He was kissing her throat.

I gazed blindly away to the seething boulders
hearing the sea's deep-bellied chaff;
a little terrier boat heading bravely west
with sails full curved like a woman's breast.
The sky had a snowing look, a serpent glare.
I looked, lacking you beyond that vast opposing flood.
I was near to heart-bursting, near to maniac laugh.
Against the swollen clouds the Bailey stood
a domed red-capped finger at heaven facing.
The gulls wrote asterisks in the air.

Below the crumbling seaweed wall the couple were embracing
dim in the heaping mist, the hooded swirl
of dull-edged foam down the bruised shore,
the man half-shielding the recumbent girl
her hair wild about his obscured face
in a brown tangle. Above the roar
of chaotic nature did I catch a sound
half strangled love, half primal pain?
Long in all that steaming gull-haunted waste
I stared down at the flattened sand where they had lain.

Sunday Morning

They troop by in twos and threes
with covered heads and uncovered knees
scented bright queenly exteriors
matted eyelashes and articulate posteriors.

In possessive suits or flaring dresses
uplifted mounds of lacquered tresses
each Sunday they come their wriggling way
to preen, to gossip, and perhaps to pray.

In garrulous groups or discreet pairs
they blithely bask in rude male stares
while this impious member of the congregation
thinks thoughts of lovely copulation.

No worthy philosophic themes
disturb my holy Sabbath dreams;
for what has Eternity to offer better
than a girl in a tight skirt and sweater?

High Noon

The girl on the beach knows nothing but sun
bearing down on her bare.

What does the large or small future hold;
will the volcano erupt;
are the sharks gathering down in the bay;
what is happening meanwhile back in the jungle;
where have all the young men gone
with all their bright young lusts;
will success spoil Mary Jordan;
is it now the time of year to put fresh flowers
on her mother's ten-year grave;
will the Moon of Manakura shine for her;
will the glow-worms glow
in the parched brown grasses of the summit
outshining the lights of the scimitar bay;
will her ship of stars sail in one fine day
bearing her starry lover across the seas;
will he have hair on his forearms;
will the lotus bloom for her;
will the herdsman whistle up the eating-dogs
and bake the breadfruit pies;
should she wear nylons in this really tropical weather
                            we're having
for that most pressing engagement tonight at eight
with the manager of the fresh-fruit factory . . . ?

The girl on the beach knows nothing but sun
bearing down on her bare.

In Passing

When you and I were there and all the world,
   joy a berry crushed between our lips,
your breast-lifting arms stretched to the sun,
   standing triumphant, toes square in the sand,
dark wing of hair blowing across your eyes
   and upon us the lovely lassitude of love.

With fingers fast-joined we held the universe in,
   laughing high and free upon the wind,
summer lightning upon our quicksilver tongues
   wild in the days of our needing,
wanton and wild the dark rush of life in us
   hectic in the plunging of our blood.

And you and I were there and all the world.

You are gone, the joy-berry of the world,
   attainment now a hard thing held in the palm,
gone the brilliant foolish talk, the singing vein
   surging to its final frantic victory.
Love now is a clean-cut conception, a logical aftermath,
   solid, stolid as a house,
passion now a covenant, an indulgence, a sophisticated exercise.
   You are here still, new, and yet no longer new,
no longer a challenge, a discovery, an ever-changing sky.
   The you that was within is gone, and so am I.
And we smile and close our eyes and are polite.
   There are no new things in our world now
to dare and bedevil us into splendid flights of folly.
   Only placid satisfied faces, trim lawns, bookshelves,
white shirt-fronts, punctual cocktails, skies with nothing in them,
   blue and vast and empty as those of an idiot.
People who say "thank you" and "do come again soon"
   and "that dress you wore to the theatre suits you very much"
and – "I *so* enjoyed your letter of the tenth . . ."

Lines out of Nowhere

You do not appear
nowhere down all the mazed days of my searching
in this autumnal spring of sorrow;

you stepped smiling and sure
out of the walled garden of my heart
into some improbable tomorrow.

My heart knows you still most intimately;
roots run deep in my garden
though I might miss your face in a crowd.

Joy played awhile with my dreams
then gravely gathered them up
in a shroud.

A little time of pleasure
but mine while time is known;
now only this I know –

that wherever you are in time
by whomsoever loved,
my heart will go

still capable of song
though faint and ineffable
as fragrance of frost.

You taught me a thing of much moment;
I did not know one could live
with life itself lost.

Abel

My brother Cain the afflicted likes to sit
brushing softly my shoulder by the water
at night's edge, or in a cinema dimlit
where scenes of peace turn to scenes of slaughter.

Sometimes he will talk to me; his voice
murmurs the commotion in his mind
and begs me to delay my final choice
and I obey, for he is wise and kind.

He shall choose the last long pain for me;
he knows the thing that must be done, my brother;
it is not treachery – our love was free,
it is no will of his or mine, but rather

the timeless tyranny of things ordained
makes life seem death and love reflected hate;
and full my heart, my sacrifice unstained:
"I wait for you, my brother, at the gate."

Meridian

She's not as beautiful as she used to be;
    there's an ageing on her
    the eye might not see
    and the still generous heart might condone;
but the mind, that merciless surveyor,
    will not be appeased by memory
of her former excellences.

The charm of her presence
    grows threadbare thin;
    her letters no longer enchant;
    she's as familar as a well-worn coat.
It is therefore sobering to reflect
    that one day I too will be forty.

Multum In Parvo

I tell you, she is all you need –
a mascara marvel, a Max Factor de Milo
streamlined and scented, without a blotch
(if you except the falsies and the rubber crotch)
but guaranteed.

Though she struts about brash and bold
in leather jacket and thigh-high boots
and whenever she feels receptive
stubbornly insists on a contraceptive –
she really has a heart of gold.

She's fit and vital and quite willing
to bring you sedatives in bed
and uncan your favourite dish
and copulate whene'er you wish
and not demand an extra shilling.

What greater love than this?
She can talk for hours without saying a thing
and your aching muscles rub
as you sit stark in a bath-tub;
what greater love than this?

You want *love?* Oh grow up!
That went out with hansom cabs
and who is there to deny
it wasn't all one bloody lie –
a tale told in a teacup?

She has enough to carry her
despite the rubberoid accessories;
no neurosis or complex
believing religiously in sex
and anyhow she is your last resort – marry her!

Inheritance

To the blandished bowl of sky
leaps the insatiable hawk
in spinning spirals of mazed enquiry
seeking the blurred hieroglyphics of its beginning.
Deafmute tongues of tongue-tied thoughts
flare across the oceanic wastes of a room
loud as an afternoon landscape
sharp as a knife in the ribs
blade-toothed serpentine whispers
lipping the crumbling ledges of my mind.

The innumerable rustles of existence
swelling visibly between the clock's death rattle
tenacious fingers of earth
pushing up through jagged pores of concrete
defying the crushing feet of men
in sing-song streets of old blind houses.
Affinity glimmering briefly, beautifully
in known never-known faces of singular strangers
in broken burning alleys of sunset.
The electric hum of creation
caught once in the satin swish
of a girl's airy dress
down an unremembered avenue.
The bleak blanched limbs of Winter
mirrored in green-weeded waters.
A voice babbling in an empty room
to drown its own dull rebellion
hemmed in by an iron heritage
of blackened chimney stacks and gaseous buses
and uncharted backyards bilge-bulging with unfed cats.

A hovel of rust-shining squalor
heaped against the sky
small impetuous beasts embroiled with love and lust
holy novenas and adultery

rabid publicans in soiled smocks
tolling out the daily ending
yellowing leaves of books
shadowed in lick-spittle corners.
A hand lightly on my sleeve
and the loneliness of being on earth.

Frostbite

I might have made a poem of this
a month, a year, a decade ago,
the bleak and broken-back garden,
the trees that died in infancy.

Now there is nothing to write about
in a morning big with thunder
and rain lashing my low wooden roof.
The savage and tender green
of the bruised grass outside my window,
the wind suddenly dying
at the far end of a cloud.
Hungry cats arched crooked over garbage bins.
The rainy smell of upturned earth
and birds falling instantly silent
down jagged steppes of sky.

I might have made a poem of this
when I was young, not long ago.
Some familiar addition
some fine fierce frenzy for life
could have made this a rounded number,
could have made this music.

Now I need only remember
this shadow falling on summer
and the silence of another
above the purple roar of thunder.

Spring

Above the reek of turpentine and linseed oil
and cabbage odours trailing from the kitchen
Spring assails my senses
and giddies my heart long schooled in winter.

Sparrows for the working man
set up a turmoil in the stunted bushes
and an out-of-bounds blackbird lords the sky
above the television spires.

I know Spring is come home
not by sight of leaf or sound of bird
but that my heart wakes from solitude
and leaps out of anguish to meet her.

My Ship

When I was a lad my bed was the ship
that voyaged me far through the star-dusted night
to lands forever beyond the world's lip
dark burning olive lands of delight
across blood-red oceans under the stars
lorded by the scarlet splendour of Mars.

And always the night was loud with the roar
of flame-nostrilled horses flying over the waves
bearing great urns of nectar to a diamonded shore
to madden fat kings and despoil obsequient slaves.
And high over the enchanted orb of my eye
bright galleons of singing men passed in the sky.

And they sang of strange things all glory and fire
of water turning to wine and men rising from dead
and I trembled with a wild and fearful desire
at things that filled me with such joy and such dread.
And their songs filled the hidden places of my heart
till part was whole and whole was part.

Climbing to bed in that lost magical time
was ascending to great secret galaxies of truth
where all meaning was couched in one singular rhyme
that would open only to the unwoken beauty of youth.
And my ship was beautiful and strong and clean
sailing to glories by the mere eye unseen.

It is only a bed now spread with eiderdown
and the sheets merciless chains holding me down.

Muted

I suffer from an impediment
of the soul;
I am a deafmute
in thought;
the loneliness of another
shouts at me in baffled hurt
across the cosmic widths of a street
above the metallic sirens of traffic
in velvet-plush wastes of lounge bars
pounding with bone-bare knuckles
upon the subtler bars of thought
begging admittance
begging heed
begging to be heard in all that wilful wilderness.
And I hear, I heed, I listen
but cannot reply
being mute
for I am without the key to either of our prisons
and the oceanic spaces roll soft and sullen
between our inlocked island souls
tossing our shipwrecked cries wearily into nowhere
and nowhere do we find a quiet shore to walk upon
and quietly discover each other
needless of the empty theatre of words;
only the impassioned impeded soul stuttering in its cage
spluttering in its rage
helpless against controls iron-clad
raging to be a moment free
eloquent and free as it was meant to be
and ah! the deafmute unuttered unutterable thoughts
broken on their brief doomed career
fall limply to earth between us
dead as any leaves in any dead season
and Despair the faithful lapdog
safe on its lonely hill

watches the human dumbshow out of old sardonic eyes
waiting to be called home
as called it will be
to the hollowed hearts of men.

Yesterday I saw a lame bird indifferently maimed
hobbling under my window
flapping its shattered wing at the sky
and its eloquence stopped my breath.

Waking

When you appeared
that ordinary afternoon
over the crumpled brow of the years
I understood only
a slow astonishment.

You came out of October
with strange beginnings in your hands
to one who had not yet had a beginning
and discerned an end in every departure.
I envied the fate of young twenty-less Chatterton
dying his incandescent death
and Keats giving his holy flesh
to Roman worms to make earth nobler.
Fire then was fire to me
love a cold flame
a static echo in the mind
no thrill in the torture
of things unrealised.

You came
and now you whip my heart to life again
with silken whips of pain.

The Lost Prize

My soul was drunk, but my mind quick
with daggered hints of truth
    the dumb rhetoric
of the unseen play behind curtained lids.
        I was sick
with stale porter and the staler dreams
        that squirmed and whimpered
in my tangled guts. Voices that held no sound
        flushed faces that simpered
in imbecilic pay-night bliss.
        Port and sherry mouths someone wanted to kiss.
Men singing In Dublin's Fair City with pipes of clay
    stuck grim in toothless gaps
        brown beer from taps
cascading into tilted tumblers;
    shawled women with puckered eyes
        and flat withered paps
whispering blasphemies in luscious asides
    soft as spider's spinning
        sharp as upthrust swords
a leaping Etna spray of words
    in the blue tobacco air
        swirling to the oak beams
        undiscovered underground seams
of burnt-out undreamt-of dreams
    crammed sweat-stuck in stall-like snugs
        as cattle on market day.

And surprisingly you came
emptied quite of praise or blame
    deep and cool as a Sunday pool
        a stillness in chiffon and lace
a pause in a mad inner dialogue of garbled eloquence
    remote, refined out of existence
a pale shimmer of knee under your dress

a half-opened volume
           your semi-smile solemn
a pint of black porter between me and that improbable heaven
           under your dark level brows.

Voices crackled on
static in the humming ether
      a backroom bar-room bedlam raucous and loud
inhuman cadences
      falling through a purple cloud
drip-drip-dropping into my bruised mind
      a lair of jungle beasts splendid and blind
blithe and brave in their doomed dust
      and useless shining warrior rust;
no behindness
      no quick of elemental lust
beyond the fatuous stare
      the drooling tender obscenities
           the gnarled ever-reaching fingers.

And you my Barrett-Browning, folded hands in lap
           a slow star across a moveless tide
a deathless dream that had already died
           so far behind my stunted life
a flowering tree lightning-cut.
           I stared dully at a vein in your foot.

Eureka Etcetera

All this quite unremarkable day
the livelong lifeless hours
I chased my thoughts over the mental fields
mice in the corn
rats in the cellar
bats in the battered belfry
up and down the niggling nooks and cantankerous
    crannies
hunting the apt phrase
groping for the apposite term
hoping for the ultimate in spleen
with you minnow-like stuck in the glue of mind-matter
spurring on my spite to horrific horizons
in hopeful vengeful quest of electric eloquence;
you the very star I once sailed under
the stake at which my life burned bright
now owlishly beyond my frail strangleholds
ripping asunder my little lucid universe
with thunder of sagacious silence;
and nowhere could I find the holy words
nowhere the fiery fulminations of poetic wrath
that would unscrew my scalded soul
and shower forth from my improbable Parnassus
the lava of my erupting ego
the coals of glowing indignation;
so all this unremarkable day
all the livelong lifeless hours
I toiled mightily as any Greek sage
in pursuit of Jupiter's thunder
till wrath itself coiled up and slumbered
ensnared in its own shackles.

Then of a sweet stupendous sudden
I found the way
knew what to say
and with satanic relief could have cried;
my dear
I could not love you *less* if I tried.

City Cameo

A quayside hovel, a tenement slum
unlikely place for Cupid to come.
And my Molly standing at the door
looks very much like a halfcrown whore.

Yet I will love my woman till Judgement Day
and keep what the dustmen can't cart away.

Possession

You, who know not wisely but too well,
    must not imagine my life single, dry,
a mirrored half-smile contemplating itself, narcissus-held;
    for under my polar-opposite star
one image fills the eye

    of my world for its joy
one bodkin stabs the flesh that is likewise the spirit
    for its awakening, to quicken with the sensitive will
the recluse soul and keep always in the pitiless gaze

    and glare of praise one princedom stark in lucid air
and islanded; so striving to attain, I gain a gift of you
    priceless in the closed commerce of mind, a bargain rare

beyond knowing; for you are all lavish and flare of delight
    that stings the encumbent soul to ecstasies of zealous pain
and I, though I have you not, have you yet more fine
    in the blue intricacies of joy
than here within the mute burden of limbs.

End

Dying is a curious thing.
Not that I have ever quite died
except briefly now and then
in a hot-headed poetic way.
There is nothing ingenious about it.
A quick dolphin-plunge
under black water
and after the first year of mourning
the daisies nod undisturbed on your grave.
I could die today with a little effort
with a well-sprung wish I could die today
quietly laughing or crying
without trumpets
without ceremony
without drawing conclusions
in Mount Jerome under the fine wet grass.

Revisited

America.
A muscular anthem.
A lust of the earth.
A cry in the mind.
A cry of triumph and fear.

From my acre of mist and musing
I daredevil my way to you again
a makeshift refugee seeking asylum unpolitic.

America.
Mr Pound's vast padded cell.
You who spewed forth Faulkner and Wolfe.
You have shot poor Lincoln again
and Whitman weeps in his sleep.

From my deep dark pool of a city
I revisit you no longer as Atlantis
yet as deeply divided under your sea of division.

America.
Give us this day your greatness.
Be gracious in your strength.
Rise O golden eagle to the sun
and by the grace of God be struck colour-blind.

From my city of little latitudes
I come on a wing and a pagan prayer
and a rageful rattle of bottles and bones.

America.
    Your summer is burning in my eyes.
I groan at your gigantic birth.
    Be less of steel and more of soul.
Pour me out a little peace.

And at the end a tired smile
    from eyes that see into my night
enough for me to see.

Brendan

He roared with that deepbellied growl of sad hilarity
   his gorgon's head and cherub's face
      swimming into view over the pint tops,
and opposite me in the bleak bar he chewed deserted gums,
   mouthing parables and paradoxes and pure plenitudes of
                                  pleasure
      in the living thunder of the moment,
the gargantuan gargler of our day with schoolboy mien.

The hallowed profanities hung in the air as incense,
   as so many Halley's comets flaming in the ether of ordinary
                                    day;
      his face swam in the smoke, a melacholy moon
in an evening sky of set stars and early rainclouds,
   a warrior of words on the last battlefield,
      toothless, untamed, untimid yet, raising the flag,
tramping towards his unmapped Timbuctoo with tired
                                truculence.

And to the literary den in Hawkins Street we adjourned,
   his blackrobed blackbird of a mother in proud awe
      and myself sweetly crooked in the wheelchair;
he pulverised Luther and Brian Boru
   and longdead Conn of the hundred heroic orgies
      and spoke with gentle garrulous Godspeed
of that decent, decadent man, the Parisian Joyce
   forever ours, in his dark watchtower on the Seine
      going blind with exile at the fag-end of his days;
a consummation he too devoutly wished,
   to be sent up in righteous flames on the Quays
      by the naive natives timorous of dying unabsolved
of their literary lusts lying dark on their little lost souls.

The harlequin of every hooley, the wonder of every wake,
   the observed of all observers, the curse of the fair state,
      shaggyheaded Pan with a song for the unbeautiful,

crowned and drowned King Puck clowning for the populace
   ribbing the ribs of the rigid righteous
       with his rash panacea of ribald rhetoric,
anointing our maimed memories with salt.

He, like another, went none too gently into that night
   from whose bourne he will always return tongue in pudgy
                             cheek,
      a rakish refugee from life's dull fanfare
peering into snugs in sad haunt of the chiding citizens he loved
      in whose cause he laboured lustily and long;
the cause of the Slate, the Beano, the Uncles,
   the bacchanalian bludgeoning of bloated John Bull,
      Moore Street dealers and the singing pubs
and the holy veneration of Liffey water.

A Glasnevin warbler was singing after hours;
   I toed the new clay on that yellow grave of laughter
      pensive in the perennial pursuit of a pint,
and him beyond the need of it and the pale panegyrics of men.

A Kind of Lament for Patrick Kavanagh

And are you gone on the whiskey-wild wind
to help push up eternal demented daisies
and count your bellyful of bruised blessings
in some fool-forsaken furrow of sky?

Out of the rancorous northland you came
on a high wind of bombast
to teach us our poetical manners
surly surgeon with sure steady scalpel
slicing through our parsimonious paeans
brushing hot crumbs off your felicitous fingers
for the rabblement to savour and savage
hawk's face flaming under black sombrero
striding with shoes untied through singing streets
of a lost city that never called you son.

Many's the brash young bard wilted
under the salty slash of your tongue
(myself included
though those were my beardless years)
scowling and growling in your cups
O monarch and messiah of McDaid's
pulverising the whelping young pups
licking your uncompromising country boots
falling into venomous daydreams
on the national television network.

Were you magnanimous?
Only as Swift was
your gleaming pince-nez in shadow
glittering into our stuttering souls
even on a rare day suffering fools
who put whiskey in expecting wisdom to come out
tramping quiet canal banks behind back

stopping to be a child again with children
emptying the gems of your unhoarded treasure
under that dense derogatory sky.

On the contrary side of the moon
I heard the wind of your passing
and that night saw a shooting star
and called it mere coincidence.

To Helen Keller

I heard it on a plain undreaming day
hunched by the squat old toadstool of a radio
that never did give out the news clearly anyway.
You had just died.

The house lay in Sunday morning silence.
Out in the dull pavement-grey day
people sulked or strutted to church
full of their little unholy terrors and persecutions.
I nursed my headful of dreary dissipation
half hearing the erratic static of the gut-twisted radio
that remote disembodied faraway stilted voice
jerking over the crammed and jammed airlanes of man-made
mayhem:
"We regret to announce the death of . . ."

I heard the news alone.
Alone when I most needed someone to share this sorrow
and yet would most certainly have resented that intrusion.
Such a sorrow is never shared
as that kind of triumph is seldom won.
I felt a momentary surprise.
Surprise that so beautiful a life should have a closing
so like any other.
As if beauty can ever know a close.

Yet I knew
and felt envious.
Envious of your life and your dying.
A symphony only you could listen to
throbbing at your fingertips like light.
A vision beyond the crazy charade of sight.
A dream torn from pain
that had in it all the music of all the birds
that ever sang in this deafmute world.

You who saw such splendour of light
heard such a marvel of music
conversed and had your being with such beauty.
You shrank my shrill little world to an atom
made me lift my eyes to pain
and not decline the chalice.

For My Mother

Only in your dying, Lady, could I offer you a poem.

So uncommonly quiet you lay in our grieving midst
        your flock of bereaved wild geese
pinioned by the pomp and paraphernalia of death
        for once upon a rare time wordless
beyond the raw useless grief of your nine fine sons
        the quiet weeping of your four mantillaed daughters
gathered in desperate amity around your calm requiem hour
        and almost I saw you smile in happy disbelief
from the better side of the grave.

Only in your dying, Lady, could I offer you a poem.

Never in life could I capture that free live spirit of girl
        in the torn and tattered net of my words.
Your life was a bruised flower
        burning on an ash-heap
strong and sure on the debris of your broken decades
        unwilting under a hail of mind-twisted fate
under the blind-fisted blows of enraged love
        turning ever toward the sun of a tomorrow
you alone perceived beyond present pain.

Only in your dying, Lady, could I offer you a poem.

You were a song inside my skin
        a sudden sunburst of defiant laughter
spilling over the night-gloom of my half awakenings
        a firefly of far splendid light
dancing in the dim catacombs of my brain.
        Light of foot and quick of eye for pain
you printed patterns of much joy upon the bare walls of my life
        with broad bold strokes of your Irish wit
flaming from the ruins of your towers.

Only in your dying, Lady, could I offer you a poem.

With gay uplifted finger you beckoned
        and faltering I followed you down paths
I would not otherwise have known or dared
        limping after you up that secret mountain
where you sang without need of voice or words.
        I touched briefly the torch you held out
and bled pricked by a thorn from the black deep rose of your
                                  courage.
        From the gutter of my defeated dreams
you pulled me to heights almost your own.

Only in your dying, Lady, could I offer you a poem.

I do not grieve for you
        in your little square plot of indiscriminate clay
for now shall you truly dance.

O great heart
        O best of all my songs
                the dust be merciful upon your holy bones

A Better Than Death Wish

Let me not go tamely out to sea
the eternal sea
the only sea
that waves us on to oblivion.

O let me rant and roar as the very waves
as always down all the bruised days of my reckoning.
Let me shout and scream and laugh and curse
and pray in the hollow rock of my penitence.

Christ, you all-seeing son of an inconceivable woman,
don't let me die between the sheets
or even between the thighs of some foolish ready woman.
Let me die with the wild wind in my few hairs
the mad Irish weather scudding over my mind
the bitter-sweet aftertaste of oaken beer
anointing my senses.

O Lord of wine and water
fire and snow
purifier and destroyer of all my days
grant me this:
that when I die
it will be under an Irish sky.

Background Music

Towards Morning

For Mab

There is a land above the wind for you to walk through
O my near and inaccessible love.
Green waves for a chariot
clouds to move as shadows about your live uplifted face.

Surf shall frolic among the toothy off-shore rocks
imperturbable background music to our dreaming
happy and lost in this new morning freedom
exquisite on our silent tongues.

Between sky and sea and sand shall be written
in broad brilliant asterisks of truth
the journey that led us unerringly towards morning
caught briefly and forever in a puzzled glance.

The stones will not hurt your feet.
You will come running down the singing shore
and step smiling and sure out of the cold clear morning
into my dream of dreams.

Drinking Song

My flesh sings a jangled rhyme of dying
crying
it sings in the pyre of its bitter burning
turning
to the grotesque gargoyle god of mangled nights and days
always
the terrier smell of my flailed flesh trails after
laughter
beating insanely against the walls of my padded cell
hell
in the last savage twisting of a cork.

Rhyme me a riddle for living.

I open the bright amber river of doom
gloom
exploding into baleful blistered light
height
mellifluously melting and spreading to sky
immensity
a burst bubble boiling and broiling in my bruised gullet
bullet
smashing into the sodden soaken marsh of my mind
blind
under the hounding hooves of oblivion.

Rhyme me a riddle for loving.

Stars dance a mad satanic dance overhead
tread
like demented fireflies in the gutter
splutter
metallic across that hell-bound space
grace

beheld briefly in a woman calmly passing
massing
clouds obscuring the bloodstained city
pity
the paltry wine of this world anointing me.

Riddle me no rhyme at all.

My flesh sings a song of jangled dying
flying
proud above the debris and the loss
cross

of broken bones against the moon.

City Dweller

I have never seen wild Donegal
nor the Atlantic cliffs of Kerry,
though in a haze of alcohol
I might have admired Enniskerry.

I've never dreamt beneath Ben Bulben's head,
or in a pool of poppies hid my face,
and the sweetest poems I have ever read
were down in Christchurch Place.

I've never looked down from the hills of Mourne
to the laughing sea at my feet
for the grandest of scents to my nostrils borne
came from the stalls in Moore Street.

Galway's glories rugged and raw
were in one single afternoon seen,
and the only lakes that I ever saw
were those in St Stephen's Green.

No call of soft-vowelled curlew
came to me across evening leas,
and all the lilting strains I knew
were in The Shaky Man's on the Quays.

Yet my Liffey dreams were just as sweet
as those in a Wicklow valley,
and my heart was first forged in Merrion Street
and blinded with love in Bull Alley.

Distance

Stars both dim and bright
candle-tips or orbs of light
swim in emptiness they say
many a billion mile away.

Many a billion mile and year
before their beam discerns us here
before their beam discerns the part
we would keep hidden in the heart.

In this tangled sphere below
heart cries out to heart I know
and one is dust for many a year
before another heart will hear.

As distant as star is from star
heart is from heart, and twice as far.

Fallen Masonry

Few things are ever mended
by mere touch of expert fingers;
no dream is ever ended
that in the lost heart lingers;
lack of love decreases
the joy of every season
and all the bits and pieces
of self sold for high treason.

We can never quite put away
that which once was ours
or surrender to the clay
the ruins of our towers;
however good the mask
we try on for disguise
we cannot help but ask
the impossible from unanswering eyes.

Each set as far apart
as star is from star
the distance of each heart
is as immeasurable and far
and the wreckage of a lifetime
is endlessly extended;
in her house, as in mine,
few things are ever mended.

Good Friday

In and out among the narrow little ways of the town
  They dragged Him, bearded Man, and the gems of sweat
On His brow glittered like gold-dust
  In the merciless fire of noon-day.
Sticks flashed and thudded dully on straining flesh;
  Taunts, maledictions, words sharp with scorn and hate
Sank as fire into the tired brain;
  Spits bright with foulness ran as lava down His chest,
And the cruel, thin stones of the hillside
  Made the blood run from the stumbling Feet,
Staining the earth with a crimson glory.

  On they dragged Him, the cross's shadow on His back,
Up the awaiting hill, as an animal to the slaughter-house.
  He gazed forlorn, with timeless pity upon the deriding
            multitude,
Sunk in the agony of betrayal, His denied majesty
  A crown of thorns girding the tranquil brow;
And there, Fatherless, they nailed Him to a beam of mountain
            wood,
  And the pain-bright eyes gazed into the deeps of all that
          had been and was yet to be,
Surveying His world, His desecrated Garden, hanging from the
            cross
  Upon a brooding hill, a bleeding Ecstasy.

Her Absence

Some red-tipped cigarette ends in the ashtray.
That painting she admired of Leeson Street Bridge
now put away in a corner out of view.
The Van Gogh she gave me to study
with an inscription from someone else inside
from her student days that made me instantly jealous.
It seems strange that only the other day
she sat in that creaking old armchair
across the cluttered-up space
smoking rather too much, and chatting,
or slim fingers pensively patting
dark-brown raven's wing of hair in place,
my hunting irreverent eyes zealous
to each line of her in that dark suit,
I for once quite still, quite mute,
the ever-changing heaven of her face
as she read my latest poem in silence
that was pure she-devil hell for me,
light copper-glinting on her bobbed hair
from the window behind her, the chair
that held her pressed-back shoulders
oh, so unconsciously!

The sudden desolate deafening quiet
in the dreaming wake of her leaving,
my heart's April-wild riot
of obscure inarticulate pain,
that uncatchable wisp of perfume
she called by some queer foreign name
lingering faintly, fatally in my room
like many a false alarm of Spring.

There's no one now to say, "take it easy,"
and discuss with mock-serious faces
the high incidence of suicide in marriage.

There's no one now to show my latest poem to
and wait for her to attack or approve
with brown eyes warm with solemn praise.
These are fiercely industrious days.
I am less interrupted now with love.

Finding

I write not in pursuit
but in memory
or in pursuit of a memory.

Something there is in me,
some tenacity
will not let things be,
will not let sleeping dogs lie
and the dead be decently dead.
It is almost an obscenity,
this twisting and turning back
into the twists and turns of the past,
this ardent archaeology of the heart
digging up buried Pompeiis of emotion,
lost mansions of affection.

Sipping iced bourbon
on a mosquito-netted back porch;
burnt caress of sand
under limbs prone in the noon;
wordless drives along white August roads
Harold Johnston motels punctuating the miles
down the pre-dawn day to Boston . . .
so long ago, time or dream
is now open to conjecture.
I am sure of so little –

but this:
the night of the open-air cinema
background music of "The Apartment"
above the crackling intercom system,
the stars a backdrop,
her warm slight body against mine
in the anonymous dark,
then home to coffee and explanations . . .
this at least remains
most blessedly unimagined.

In Retrospect

When you walked down that street
on ordinary feet
no trace of angelic grace
hallowed your pensive face
and your hair, although quite nice,
was not beyond the price
of a beautifying lotion.
And I had no hint or notion
that down that asphalt street
on quite ordinary feet
under a factory-smoke sky above
came the epitome of love.

For what books had never told me, dear,
and what I never knew
was that, when the great day came, dear,
love would be merely . . . you!

In the Theatre Box

All the while they discussed the new play
her eyes explored me;
and when they arose to go
her dress rustled like old leaves
down an avenue of another October.

Invocation

I voyage out
from this embattled colony of thought
to where you rise always upon a moveless tide
always as morning.

This eyeless night of bleak dimensions
cannot kill the brief splendour I knew
the forked fire in my marrow
where you flamed.

From these raw sad inarticulate ghosts
the stunted statuary of my life
you draw me past time and time's dull tyranny
into the harbour of your look.

And I enter quietly sweeping and singing
a small secret song inside my skin
to where your shadowed smile finds me out
in a room full of ordinary mortals.

Reading the unfolding of my fate
in the fine calligraphy of your veins
O long before I knew I was alive
to that high art and most singular pain.

Raging in my bones I called your name:
Joy came.

Last Post

I knew the writing immediately
on the letter,
knew the hand more intimately
than the back of my own;
so many times before had I known
that dry, laconic style
that somehow matched her smile –
it hadn't changed a bit,
and the criss-crossed envelope
with sorrowful Lincoln on it
at a crazy slope
stacked with pages that spoke
of writer's cramp; I broke
the seal and read
the things her heart had said.

It began without preamble –
that too was typical
in lines unlyrical;
recapitulations
of scenes shared – the hectic scramble
of morning classes – afternoons spent
in intellectual argument –
solemn declarations
of mutual hates – grave promises –
loaning of books – rebellious Luther
and ascetic Aquinas – discussing a future
we both believed in – sworn dedications –
no trucking with compromises!

But with time
and time's implications –
for no reason or rhyme –
we had had our innings –
farewells and fresh beginnings –

letters put off – communication
gone stale, unused,
old loyalties abused –
the fierce convictions revoked –
the old free commerce choked –
the insidious infusion
of new blood – unvoiced suspicion
of the past – the gradual intrusion
of personal lives –
husbands, wives –
security, maternity, ambition –
ultimate separation.

We had never bargained for such grim mutations –
yet it was but to be expected –
too taken for granted and neglected –
our trust had destroyed the relation.

Lines for Lioba

On her first visit

I

The small flowers you brought
the morning of your leaving
are a week of age this morning
yet they fill my room still
most sweetly, most eloquently
and bring to my saddened mind
your gentleness strong as flowers
breathing out of your silences.

II

Your hands stirred then;
delicate white petals in your lap
against the soft leaf-brown dress.

III

Your gentleness disarmed me;
pointless my arrows fell
in the clear path of your gaze.

IV

You said little;
we broke from the net of words
the black forest of chosen language
free and familiar upon the bright strand
of our understanding
happy and wise as only we can be
who demand nothing of each other;
we looked with eyes not in our heads
and were not dismayed.

V

The small truth you brought with the flowers
grows strong-rooted in crevices of my heart;
not now forever can you escape into unremembrance;
not now forever can knowledge of you be lost
in a trap of time;
as a flower in my mind you shall grow
and time is kind to flowers.

Lines of Leaving

I am losing you again
all again
as if you were ever mine to lose.
The pain is as deep
beyond formal possession
beyond the fierce frivolity of tears.

Absurdly you came into my world
my time-wrecked world
a quiet laugh below the thunder.
Absurdly you leave it now
as always I foreknew you would.
I lived on an alien joy.

Your gentleness disarmed me
wine in my desert
peace across impassable seas
path of light in my jungle.

Now uncatchable as the wind you go
beyond the wind
and there is nothing in my world
save the straw of salvation in the amber dream.
The absurdity of that vast improbable joy.
The absurdity of you gone.

Looking at a Photograph

God, you looked young!
Yourself and myself outside the United Nations
that glass menagerie of caged animals
that citadel of the world's foolish hopes
that doomed Notre-Dame
with all the world as its hunchback.

I always did admire you in yellow.
It somehow brought out the wild lostness in you
the gay deeply caring forever-young in you
willing to walk forever with a dream.
The fountain behind us was a puny thing
compared to the torrent that quietly raged within us.

The sun was so obvious that day.
It shone through your dress
and rendered me happily blind.
Boats were sighing down the river
cars streaking by in an endless scream
and we alone in our world.

I am indeed alone now
looking across the cluttered spaces of my room
at that captured moment of a happier time
when time was not measured by the heartbeats of a clock
and I did not have to measure my joys
by how much I had left in the bottle.

Lucy

She came clouded in mystery and mysticism
and white Tyrolean stockings
from blue Alaskan wastes
to my city of little infinities
her Joan of Arc countenance flushed
in the fervour of her cosmic faith.

She wrote dreamily for children
of animal simplicities
and golden fireflies dancing above brimming buttercups
and buttermilk afternoons and streams that sang
and a God perched prettily on a tree
in a flowing robe of amethyst.
Not of this world was Lucy-in-Wonderland.

She taught me cosmic acceptance
of all things kind and tragic
marvellously vague and indefinite
her fragile thoughts swimming in cosmic oblivion
desiring nought, possessing all
well versed in Francis Bacon and Annie Besant
her rosy Rosicrucian soul blooming in her eyes.

I heeded her sadly;
there was a nunnery odour about her
that bred despair in me
devoted to her long-dead Bacon
another citadel unstormed
another paradise lost
and I savage and intent
marooned with my lonely passion
barred from that final haven
by a pair of holy-white Tyrolean wool stockings.

What has since become of her
my frail American evangelist
with the lustrous eyes and John-Brown spirit
only God knows
and He isn't perched on any tree.

Meeting

For E. O'K.

Daydreaming it down Henry Street
oblivious of the thronging feet
eyes downcast and remote
dark glimmer of fur about your throat
under a dense, dull December sky
passing me by, passing me by.

Passing me by without look or word
without the merest trace of regard
your Hellenic face hidden behind a cloud
moving like one in an ancient shroud
quiet, deliberate and sad of eye
passing me by, passing me by.

Then you turned and your eyes
found me there in some surprise
and you came back to where I waited
a poor man's Prometheus bound and fated
your eyes alive again, brilliant and fine
you back from your dreaming, I lost in mine.

Lady, step always with sagacious feet
among the temptations of Henry Street.

Poem for Sean Collis

For Han and Bob

You who went so innocently before us
do not forget us in that green-gold world of yours.
You the gay laugh upon the Wicklow wind
smiling boy upon a rainbow
galloping over the morning of your life
blessedly unmet with crippling remembrances
shaming us with your enthusiasms.
Spare us now a thought of quiet love
in all your fourteen-year-old wisdom
you whom death has so dismally failed to possess.

You will always enter through the farmhouse door
laden with clean-cut turf for the fire
bearing warmth of young heart
bearing tokens rare beyond your knowing
for those who knew you too briefly
and loved you too well for jealous time to suffer
yet had unkillable joy in that knowledge.

Gather still turf for that unending fire
from your brighter side of the river
joining us all so improbably as one
over a candle-lit table far from last supper
bridging lives once stellar in distance
through the firefly flaming of your youth
and its dark tongueless ending.

I did not know you well, knowing only your eyes.
And knowing your eyes, knew you.
In some other better time boy on rainbow
beyond the brittle dimensions of now
sup with me again at the same table
and crumble between us the bread of brothers.

Sean of light gentleness and boyish wayward ways
the cloud that darkens your last green hour
hangs over us all.

The Drink

She sat there cosily beside me
twining her slim glass in her fingers
hip against mine in the small booth
in out of the December fog and frost
icy streets and rooftops of cars parked outside.
We sat hip-touching, cosily dreamily drinking
in the merry-making midst of the local citizenry;
bricklayers, carpenters, truck drivers, boilermen
and men of praiseworthy unemployment
downing black-skirted cream-topped pints of stout
like avaricious fishes full to the gills,
in randy currents of man-talk about women,
men with grown-up daughters discussing with phallic famine
the attributes of grown-up daughters of other men,
a geyser-shower of bluer-than-blue jokes
flung prodigally into the smokey air,
true men one and all hunched at the Killiney-rock bar
in varying attitudes of stilted eloquence
becoming less stilted, more slurred with beer;
sloping shoulder, half-moon face,
eyes squinted in comic disbelief, hand slapping corduroy thighs,
bedroom intimacies leaking and lisping
from behind mouth-concealing hand, heads nodding
                                                    emphatically,
wouldn't tell a word of a lie
and herself big-bellied as usual at home
making the lunch for the morning.
The talking ball tossed back and forth unendingly
like ganseyed kids up a handball alley.

She sat there cosily beside me
twining her glass in her prayer-like hands
hip against mine in the small booth
looking for a moment absurdly and incongruously nun-like
in her dark ankle-length coat and dark scarf.

We sat there till closing time
and only out in the cold and fog and frost
did I realise we hadn't said a word.

Mutability

There is a higher world than this far and strange
    where loving hearts are subject to no change
out of our narrow day, the blinkered mind
    where no rude remembrance leaves behind
a sour taste on the tongue;
                there no shadows move
the hushed eternal expectancy of love
    and there above the thunder and the rain
unending love brings no unending pain;
                in that place
love alters not with the changing face
    but lives forever conquering in grace
            imperishable, unspoiled, unsaid –
and dead . . .

And we below who can but understand
    the quick electric magic in the hand
weave our little dreams and blithely go
    out into the dark of life to know
a brief fugitive pleasure
              and bravely kiss –
and think life holds little else than this –
    the faint sweet intimacy of fingers
lulling us into spells; nothing lingers
    save a scarecrow limping sorrow in the night
and soon that too diminishes and dies
    in strong questing hearts and morning eyes
opening unto new and broader light.
    It is a truth no willing lips can cover –
mortal love dies with the mortal lover
    and we are disenchanted, perplexed and sad –
and glad.

My Brothers

I have eight of them,
> some with excellent kind wives
>> endlessly embroiled in maternity;
others sweethearting a little wearily;
> they leave their thoughts undisturbed
>> and resolve disputes with fists
occasionally broken-skinned
> with the laying of Dublin bricks
>> cemented with less than love;
they talk soccer and mark the form
> of fillies both equine and feminine
>> and fidget behind white collars;
they splutter like candle-wicks
> flaring, swearing, roaring to lascivious life,
lovely white violence erupting
> in quiet pub corners out of reason
>> devoid of malice veiled or meaning;
they rant rebel themes intrepid,
> observe the faithful observances with middle fervour,
>> eyes glued to clocks for opening time;
half-drunk, half-dreaming, half in love
> they pause, rarely, to peep like mice
>> through the bamboo of their souls,
creep as marvellous jungle creatures
> through the forest of their unacted deeds
>> in proud profundity of valour;
in words splendid and unprintable
> they importune their special demons
>> to fire their loins with strength
for their not insignificant job of creation: pro.

They walk straight in the sun,
> plunder their senses prodigally,
>> hesitate about being too cautious,
copulate whenever they can;
>> but most of all they talk.

My Credo As Of Now

I conclude
   all conclusions are superfluous
full stops that never stop in one spot long enough
   to be duly devoured by logic;
truth is forever around the next bend;
   look into the honest face of an imbecile
and therein lies the reflected vacuity of oneself
   mirrored in undiscerning depth and immense;
blissful is the imbecile possessing nothing
   save intimacy of the smallest embryonic pulse
in the tremendous minutiae about him
   which might well be truth beyond assertion
the living of which strides stridently on to madness
   and is therefore worthy of our devout pursuit.

I conclude
   love enters through the eyes
trembles awhile at the fingertips
   and departs as soon as the mouth is opened;
for love's success the taking off and putting on of garments
   is not nearly as efficacious as the putting on
and taking off of masks; the best lovers are clowns.

I conclude
   the hope of every honest man is phallic-cored
and the beauty of one woman is always unequal
   to the beauty of the next;
fortunately for poets.

I conclude
   each existence is a casual tragedy
or an indifferent comedy as the case may be
   sustained only by images of hell
and the last sad lugubrious truth
   that there isn't a damned thing to know except nothing.

My Mother's Son

I suffered long before life taught me
the necessity of hypocrisy –
how you must bend your face to the earth
and your protesting soul to the sobbing earth
though you wander among the stars.
I have some ancient battle scars
to show for those kindergarten days
and some not so ancient.
When I had a God to blame and praise
it wasn't so bad – I was complacent
about the things life did to me
not knowing it was the gaping gaps in my mind
and the black Calcutta holes in my mind
that were to blame for my misery,
my stunted, deaf-mute humanity.
Life is uncompromising.

To know this is to bear it
with a certain slow irony,
a flung-to-the-sky frenzy
with lips tight-pressed against blame,
for there is no culprit to name
but ourselves when nobody's in,
nobody to watch us commit the last sin
and turn away from ourselves, for this
is the ultimate cowardice.

The lapping surf of darkness
eats away into my fearing soul
and when there's no convenient God to enrol
into your category of blame,
you feel at last your own littleness.
Our self-deceit will never be done.
Yet I hope, pluck hope from nowhere
as a child that picks poppies for her hair

and sings to herself when it's quiet.
I am not very brave, and by it
I mean I'm not a silent self-suffering one.
I am my Mother's son.

Nemesis

Somewhere in my mind a demon stalks
at once reassuring and destroying.
With demonic intent it heightens my perception
of a midsummer leaf
a Chinese embroidered teacup
the svelte stripes on an aloof cat
secure in its feline nirvana
rejecting people.
And with the same singular dynamism
my most singular and insatiable demon
narrows my perception to zero
leaves me islanded in oceanic nothingness
blind eyes forever upon some insurmountable peak
till the smallest atom of dust upon the floor
or swaying in the insubstantial spaces of the day
assumes the majestic finality and terror of beginning and end.

Somewhere in my mind a demon prowls
ravaging the last remnants of my sensibilities.
Turning my faltering self to stone
it hoists me high on a makeshift cross
a prey to every season of self-doubt
tossing my mind about with cruel gay abandon
hectic in the haphazard ways of desire.
I speak a thousand tongues faultlessly
with my own farce of a tongue
caught immutably in my own image.
I speak the greatest nonsense known to suffering man
from the dismal dredges of sunken sense
and catch on a rare moment the early morning hope
of something around the corner
behind the oriental blinds
beyond the canalled skein of my closed eyelids
groping towards light.

And I know my demon well
beyond the calling of its name.
A sweet pestilence inside my skin
skying me to Icarus heights
on wings already melting
plummetting me to depths familiar beyond the telling.
My demon is myself and I my demon
joined inescapably in the one shroud of skin.

And come morning I awake to find
the old bastard ruling in my mind.

Poem on a Monday Morning

At least the clock has not expired.
That at least kept faith.
There was a dead fly in that night-long glass of whiskey
and you drank it for the best of all reasons;
there was damn all else to drink.
And now that drowned departed parasite
is now presumably swimming deep in your tangled guts
forever lost in its fly-blown nirvana.
A dreary enough final resting place
even for an inebriated fly.

Pyjamas-less you sit, Gandhi-wise, in the cardinal-red chair
your jaded genitals drooping like dead poppies
on unseen view for the girl who never loved you
gliding back across blanched lawns on razor-keen swings of
                                            lisping song
that suburban Beatrice of your mad-cap harbourless middle-
                                                        years
smiling that sublimely stupid mildly-mad midsummer smile of
                                                        hers
her strong lean tanned turbulent thighs
casually catapulting you to perdition
over the static of transistorised mayhem
and salmon sandwiches squashed in the sand.

Your thoughts now are demented eels wriggling in a shredded
                                            net
slipping and sliding coldly down the thin coil of your memory.
Monday should be a null and void thing struck from Gregory's
                                            calendar.
It offends against civilised taste. It has a sour-beer stench.
It is miniature Judgement Day for hardworking honest
                                            debauchees
rising naked and Saint-Vitus-struck from our sea-tossed sheets
and assiduously avoiding mirrors.

And that which led us so gaily into full-bosomed temptation
is now a raging volcano rumbling in our ravished bellies.

Grey is the mood and cemetery-grey the colour of the mind
in this sunken undersea world of Monday morning
where even the glad sounds of children at play
grates along the nerves like the scraping of a rusty gate.
And tumbling all crumpled from the womanless bed
the one gleam of promise to hit your inflamed eye
was the over-night tumbler of waiting whiskey
tabernacle of doom and salvation
with that doomed and unmourned fly aswim in its amber depths
butchered in bacchanalian glory.

Yet the clock kept faith and vigil.
It has not ceased speeding up your days.

Rainbow in Exeter

Like all tourists we had to find the cathedral.
Like all tourists we failed.
On the bridge we asked a fine stout open-faced Devonshire
                                        bobby the way
and stopping the traffic no doubt impressed with your candidly
                                        lost American accent
he gave us directions which we of course blissfully failed to
                                        carry out
and ended up once more at yet another petrol station
                                        asking directions.

Round and round we went as in a squirrel cage
seeking God knows what road
I dehydrated as ever coveting all the gorgeous pub signs
you stopping again and again to pore over the Esso map
and seek to trace with finely pointed fingernail our ultimate
                                        destination
on that sad penultimate day.
With absurd yet amused irritation I watched your face
bent studiously over the map spread upon your knees
and I reminding you that the lights had turned green.
The English sky was smiling most blandly overhead.
Set fair, I thought, set fair.

And then a distant voice in the sky
a distant gentle awakening behind the sudden clouds
a fine graffiti of raindrops on the windscreen
and we both of us looked up a bit startled
at the phenomenon above us.

A gateway! A glorious gateway
opening there above us beyond this traffic-loud moment
a triple-barred rainbow to another land
spreading over acres of sky
welcoming us through
and for us then it was the only true thing in the world.

Laughing, half crying, we passed through that gate in the sky
glorious in the knowledge of ourselves
not having any directions
but sure of our way.

Sunday Sequence

I

A boy and girl walk homeward
their little hour of thigh-white love
quite finished.

II

Half across her in wild Glencullen grass
his nicotine fingers flattering
her buttercup throat
brushing nipples bristling under silk,
thinking it time to say something;
saying nothing.

III

In bed malingering on Sunday morning
rasher-and-egg morning of thronging feet outside
exodus of worshippers from the beehive houses;
sister's nightshroud thrown across bed
redolent of his guilt
recalling white-mice skin of her peeping through
on the whiskey-murdered midnight
blotting out the innocent lust
leaping in wild earth.

IV

Late for Mass per usual! his Mother's voice
trailing him down the street
the Via Dolorosa of the concrete jungle,
the girls articulate in every bone
smiling at the slaughter of conscience;
late for last Mass per usual
but in time for the First Session.

V

"Speak to me, love!"
her cry unspoken because speechless
nibbling at the edges of his mind,
he answering with phallic eloquence only
bruised and breathless in chains of mute passion.
He gazes in dregs of porter, seeking omens
his Ides of March upon him.

VI

Belching home evicted from bar
to cabbage and crubeens greenly afloat
on an inner sea of potent porter;
the afternoon a desert without horizon,
his Mother at fire sewing sock over bottle,
sister curled shell-wise on horsehair sofa
deep in simulated fervour of romance novelette,
dark-silk knees just hidden under skirt
moving furtively, soft rabbits in a wood.

VII

"Speak to me, love!"
that other cry from other mouth unspoken
dropping dully into his mind
a dull plop! of raindrop on mud
signifying nothing but the boredom of being together.
She had looked for flowers
walking down the quiet ways from the mountains,
gentian-red roses everdropping from the walls
of the genteel dwellings,
pricked her thumb on a thorn, cried softly into herself,
he with blind face sleepwalking at her side
stepping blindly down into doom
into the bejewelled bowels of the night city
home to that without a name.

VIII

Christ above his bed gazing down
a sad beggar with hands oozing blood and love;
the red lamp of the Virgin
shedding doom's light on white shoulder of sister
rising above sheet in banal beauty of doom
his spider-soul caught in the web of her growing;
a milkdray rumbles down in the dead street
horse splashing urine, anointing the dawn.

IX

A boy and girl walk homeward
Their little lucid hour of thigh-white love
quite, quite finished.

Sunday Visit

We finally found him
curled up in the chair like a many-wrinkled shell
staring blindly out at nothing
among a gathering of imbecilic fossils
his one good eye fastening fiercely onto life
the hair still sturdy though silver under the old cloth cap.

We finally found him
through all that terrible labyrinth of grey concrete cells
quietly rounding out his days
alone in a morass of moronic camaraderie
his doomed cellmates snoozing and snoring all around
and he with his one good eye defying the shadows.

The tears came then
not soft, but real
the tears of a real man broken by life
groping wildly with gnarled fingers at the straws of life
in that awful room of no life
and the television set blaring forth its banalities
drowning whatever words of comfort our futile tongues could
offer.

I had no words for him
no words to span the heartbreak of years
when Samson-like he had stood between us and chaos
bringing to us the small rare trinkets of his love.
I had for him only whiskey
the old bitter gift
the poor tribute of one poorer in spirit
than that jaded near-blind half-deaf soul reclining so tamely
in a wicker chair
in a ward of fearful paralysing resignation
a ward full of already dead people
sleeping as the television blared.

Yet the hand that gripped mine spelled out love
and the raw lovely courage of that old landscaped face
put my feeble pity to shame.

The History Teacher

How shall I ever face her –
How can I disguise
The longing to embrace her,
The unwise knowledge of my eyes?

To burrow in mouldy old books
Devised for the mind's high learning,
When I can't forget her good looks
And the heart in me that's burning!

O strength! Let me be able
To master my amorous seizure,
While Cleopatra sits at my table
And talks on and on about Caesar . . .

The Night Before The Morning After

For Anne

I find myself at the old game
the old absurd ecstatic folly-ridden game
of trying to guess your mind
caught up once more in the eternal question-jungle:
"Will she come?" "Won't she come?" "Maybe not."
One half of me says you will be true to yourself
and lose your way once again.
Another and the more naïve bit of me assures me
you will arrive come hell or stale porter
blaming me as ever for woeful misdirections
and in effect saying with brown-eyed refinery:
"Why the hell pick such an outlandish place to live?"

And no doubt I shall be wordless in your presence
if you can imagine such a phenomenon
and as we self-consciously attempt to pick up long-loosened reins
my eyes upon you will be playing the old remembered ballet
under the heavy drink-laden dream-laden weight of years
almost embarrassing you into temporary disarray.
You won't be fooled, however, knowing me well;
as always you will see beyond the quick foolish clown's mask
far beyond the ready bottle of release, the straw of salvation
the real body alone in his microscopic dust
dreaming dreams forever far beyond his station
studiously looking away from you.

Yet let the old motto endure.
Drink and be merry, for tomorrow we may think.
And that could well spell disaster.

In anticipation of tomorrow
I hope the pleasure we have always found in each other
will outwit the ever-eager hawk of remorse.

Girl, bravely fool me with that old brown-eyed witchcraft
blinding me to the lesser losses of life
and guiding my reason towards the greater humbler gain.

My wish for you upon this wary midnight:
May your life be a warm attendance of light.

The Visit

You came into my night again, Mother,
with quiet undemanding suddenness
hallowing my sleep
hushing the wild drumbeats of my heart
your gentle articulate presence
more real and in life at that deeper-than-death hour
than the bleak barren walls of my mausoleum.

Your face held the broken landscape of my life
fissured with the fierce craters of your love.
Your unfamiliar muteness hung about you as a shroud
in that deeper-than-life hour
knifing me back into life
to meet again the meaner little dying of every day.

I woke down the dark to early morning
to the cold too-new anguish of your absence
bound in the winding sheet of grey normality
and searched in all my blind and bleeding world
for the rare reassurance of your ghost.
And found only my own
absurdly alive
jabbering in a hovel of ruined days.

The Wait

She won't come tonight, old boy.
Tomorrow night, maybe, or some other night
she'll come into my squat untidy room
having driven hazardously through town
and as usual lost her way.
She'll sit across from me in her favourite chair
the one that laments with her every movement;
she'll toss off her spotted scarf
shake out her massed hair
look around as always for the non-existent ashtray
and smoke with her pale pink lips
hand finger-tapping her knee.

She'll read my latest poems,
with bent studious face examine what I have written
in all those desert days since her last visit.
She'll listen as I grow loquacious
listen attentively to my arrogant themes
on life, love and the government;
in our pauses the damn clock will chirrup insanely
like crickets in high grass.

In the backwash of our silences I'll watch her
with slow burnt-out eyes;
the shadows live about her mouth.
her toes nearly visible in the thin red shoes.

Windy Interlude

For Anne:
County Antrim

On that ribbon road in the hills
you wool-jacketed against the heathery wind
above the river and the rock-jumping children
we dissected the bones of old hurts
smiled gravely at ancient beliefs now fallacies
told ourselves brave unhappy things
in sudden audaciousness of heart
I seeing not the uncertain sky
but the ever-changing heaven of your face
my heart glutted on this wonder
you most near, the singing and the gold
and the falling away of things into peace.

The first slow raindrop touched my cheek;
I did not heed at all
peacock-proud by you and incandescent
this moment never to be betrayed
never to be trodden by random treason
a flower on this leaden earth;
your head was bare
leaving your hair to blow in the wind;
upon your sudden remote face O then
a look of immense understanding
as if you knew why the day turned traitor
and the curlew's cry died even as we heard it.

You did not see me then;
something deeper held captive your eye and heart
and made the wild impetuous word die upon my tongue.

Wishful

I want to be free of pavements
and clocks that bully my existence,
newspapers, cars that whisk me like God
descending unexpectedly on me,
buses moving like lugubrious elephants.
I'm tired to death of here, my room,
this spluttering absurd monster-machine
its hammer-strokes recording for posterity
my mind's sudden audaciousness.
I would gather around me soft-sandalled things,
shadows on a burnished lake,
trees bending to the earth in love.
Where, oh where are the beautiful people,
the quick of wit, the clowns who spit
in life's sanctimonious countenance –
the insolent, the indolent, the gay
with sunlight dripping from their hair?
Bus queues, elephantine trucks, merciless clocks
and cheese sandwiches . . .

I'd pawn my immortal soul to wake suddenly
and find a girl's footprints in dew outside my door.

Young Charm

I saw her standing in the rain
eyes dull with hope and pain,
like a scarecrow standing there
a tattered scarf round her hair,
a bottle of meths drained to the dregs,
skirt clinging to mudsplashed legs,
trying to sell her wasted allure;
I hadn't the guts to look at her.

Anne

You came from out the nowhere of the past
with dead leaves in your hands,
and I who had known you alone and near
was dumb in a turmoil of speech.

You came out of a confusion of people
with new flowers in your hands
from out the blue and old gold of October
and I had found you again, but not alone.

At Caragh House

Sitting convivial and confessional
on the sunsplashed afternoon porch
the green cloak of Kildare wrapped around us
drawing our minds together sweet and sure
in a season gone beserk with beauty
under the blaze of Easter
prodigal in its mercies.

Thinking ourselves free
sipping brief peace from the bottle at our feet
passing from hand to flashing hand my ragged bits of poems
under that improbable sky
making a brilliant sunburst of your hair
spilling about your face.

We spoke brave foolish things about ourselves
dissecting life with marvellous dexterity
reckless with that moment's truth
I vainglorious as ever
glorying in your praise.

Only later did I remember the hawk
shadowing the sun
waiting, waiting.

At Closing Time

At closing time
all in the prime
of damp roses and wine
the girl slim-hipped
moist-lipped
wolf-haunted
undaunted
stepped out then
from the beehive of men
pressed her gin-and-lime mouth to mine
hair rare and fine
as blown silk against my face
there in that babel place
outside the pub
the unceasing hub
of the night-lit city
in haste without pity
flowing garishly past.

Her lips, soft, then fast
away into the anonymous night
out of blurred sight
a girl unnamed, unknown,
a stray pebble thrown
into the whirling pool of my mind
leaving behind
no cock's-comb gladness
only a sadness
for what I did not know.

I watched her go,
heard the male talk begin.
the braggart boast of sin.

Yet still the aftertaste of gin
recalls for me
haphazardly
her mouth upon mine
crushed roses and wine
and the low keen of despair
in the wild of her hair.

A Dirge Yet Not A Dirge

Let me look up at the sky
for there's still many a good reason why
I don't particularly want to die.

I keep remembering in rhyme
things that are no more in time
and drowning my sorrows in gin and lime

and thinking of things I'd like to see
under heaven and over the sea
before dull Maturity catches up on me;

A Moore Street "daler" complete with barrow
marching down the straight and narrow
cultured corridors of Harrow;

Pubs with doors that never shut;
literary debates in a watchman's hut
humour shining through grime and soot;

motors fitted with noiseless throttle;
no schoolboy made to read Aristotle;
my best poet friend off the bottle;

girls in wide Summer frocks seen
stretched under the sun in Stephen's Green
healthy and nubile and un-lesbian.

And I would put to the metaphoric sword
the gentlemen of the Censorship Board
until they gave up being Our Lord.

And foreign film-makers who stand
in our green and pleasant land
and show us all to be a pigsty brand.

Oh! for a return to the heroic mood
where every child shall have its food
and every man his favourite nude;

when nobody emits a pious shrill
when somebody gets a vicarious thrill
from their copy of Fanny Hill

and nobody with horror looks
upon those who read proscribed books
and start grappling for them with holy hooks.

And those garrulous young scribes who boast
– let them talk less and work the most
and quit waiting for the Holy Ghost.

A return to the simpler joys
that used to exist between girls and boys
before the advent of the Showband noise;

running barefoot along Dollymount strand
hair in the wind and hand in hand
cooking horse-chestnuts in the sand;

time enough to browse and dream
over a lemonade or ice-cream
fishing for pinkers in a rocky stream;

paddling in water that was shallow
sucking a liquorice or marshmallow
and long, long short-cut through the Hollow.

Ah Time, you unreliable toy!
Even my most innocent pleasure you destroy;
now there's no telling girl from boy.

Yet I must resist the urge
to tether on the tearful verge
and flounder in a soulful dirge

and there's no use grunting like a sow
or a melancholy cow;
the time is always here and now,

so let me be no stone-caster
and though these times may move faster
remember: it's not the station, but the stationmaster.

So let me look up at the sky
for there's still many a good reason why
I don't particularly want to die.

A Lesson Unlearned

Now descends the broad disenchantment
of these thirty-three far-flung years;
the solitary re-enactment
of all I failed to do
but dreamed of most fervently;
things I only half-knew
intensely
in some unvisited corner of my mind
that awoke
when the spell broke
to fantastic star-sprung fears
unabsolved by rite of years;
the brilliant and blind
visions that led on
till deceit itself was done
and my little dog-day won;
the comfortable delusions
willingly believed,
the heartscalding confusions
tortuously conceived
clearing from turgid mist and gleam
to brittle morning beam
showing up the stark
emptiness of my dark.

The ageless battle of ideals
fought across a bar-room table;
useless eloquence unable
to break the thinnest ice;
silk-hissing skirts and stiletto heels
echoes of a paradise
forever coveted and uncaught;
the Arctic wilderness of thought
leading howling on to nowhere;
love encountered here and there

turning from exquisite uncandid eyes
to a sordid compromise;
the endless folly of growing wise
hoarding jealously to ourselves
like volumes unopened on undusted shelves
much knowledge and little faith,
attaining man's high estate
hollowed-out versions of what we
once upon a wild time used to be,
before Reason took its toll
of heart and soul
leaving only the hawk that delves
into any metaphysical hole;
how casually we commit the murder of ourselves!

Yet see how little of wisdom I have learned
for while my several little Romes burned
and love itself was stranded and lost
bitten by a bitter frost,
most illogically I continue to sing
of Love, the only lovely thing.

After-Meeting

When our little rounded moment is done,
When we are far beyond the sun
Of this, our immediate day,
With idle tears and idle fears
We will not grope the airy way,
Plaintive for earth and the kind
Of dreaming we have left behind;
Rather hold hands and run
Down some windy avenue of the sky,
Till some shining corner lie
Awaiting us, and have the fun
Of rolling stars across the floor
To thunder at the Great One's door.
And then, tiring, we will go and find
Some lonely valley between cloud and wind,
Some echoing ghost-beloved nook,
And there, together, read the book
Of that other time-remembered life,
And seek the purpose in the strife,
The pain, and the astonishment,
Why it came and what it meant.
And in the pastures of the sky
We will find ourselves, you and I,
And think each in each, wondrous wise;
Learn that which now the world denies,
And feel, and know, and touch, and see
That which our mortality
So enviously debars
With the opposition of the stars;
And, beyond them, we will find
The sweet conjunction of the mind.
To have, and hold, and know, and say,
And feel, who have laid our hands away,
And see the beauty that never dies,
No longer blinded by our eyes!

So we will weep no idle tears,
Or hurt our hearts with idle fears,
When our little hour is done
And we are far beyond the sun.
There is no need for such, when we
Are ourselves for all eternity.

How to be Bored in Paradise

The sheer monotony of the beauty
just one beautiful day after another
can be rather wearing on one's nerves
even when one is in love.

Looking out at eternal palm trees
and blue blue skies
and hearing the hum of the air-conditioning
can make even the most original couple less original
waiting for the unseen presence
just waiting
is the most boring thing in the world.
Excuse me while I yawn.

Honeymoon

Herself and me not being quite ourselves
under the palm trees and those eternal mosquitoes
which is not at all ourselves
Sunshine every day as prescribed
and us pining for Irish rain
and the weather that draws people from extremes
under an everlasting sky of everyday everydayness
that is known to us alone
therefore we pine for that sky.

For Prince

We met on different sides of the world
boy on a rainbow
yours the better world of innocence
unknown to our meaner fears.

Boy on a rainbow
making our day good and clear
a life unperceived by our atrophied vision
smiling kindly at our ineptitude.

We did not know you with our slight minds
we only glimpsed the rare beauty of the truth
shaming us into the hollow shells of ourselves
much too painfully true to be good.

Dear smiling boy on a rainbow
I see you still standing on the happier side of us
giving us new knowledge of this life
as you held out your hand for a candy.

You will always be with us in the better part of our dreaming
the dark incomprehensible beauty of you
stirring us to efforts beyond our strength
hoping to catch a glimmer of your flame.

You are gone now to a sunnier someplace
and yet you will never be gone
for you are forever in the wind and in the fall of the leaf
and these endure beyond the fragile mind of men.

Boy on a rainbow
in your heaven look kindly on us objects of clay.

On the Beach

For Mab

On the beach today I saw a look of quiet amusement
pass over your skyward-turned face
as if predicting my very next word.

I held out bravely; not a predictable word
escaped my salt-watered lips for at least a minute
as I gravely contemplated the crab in the sandhole.

The sun came out like a warrior
assaulting our fragile skins.
Behind my closed eyelids it veered crazily.

Still I knew you waited so quietly in the sand
for the obvious daily words to gush from me
unstoppable as the weather itself.

The crab wore out its welcome
became assimilated with so much sand.
And still I knew that look was on your face.

No respite from the fierce delight of the sun
no respite from the fiercer joy of you
waiting, waiting quietly by my side.

You won the race for the heart.
Your silence was forever eloquent
so unlike my tortured quest for speech.

Twisting over in the sand
love almost turned to anger because you knew me so well
I almost snarled the lovely words out:

"I love you."

And your eyes mirrored the deeper beauty of it all.

Sitting

Sitting with you in any setting is so lovely
it is still so new to me like each new morning
watching each new wonder cross your face
and I a new arrival to joy
happily caught in that wonder.

Your every movement arrests my mind
bringing my senses instantly awake
and in your very stillness I am aware
of things waving my life restfully
to a joyous conclusion.

Of Snails and Skylarks

Sunset Star

Girl in the wind
blowing wide open
the closed doors of my life –
which way are we going?

Standing against the lurid sky
on the stark brink of ocean
arms outstretched
as if your love and hunger
would embrace the world
and I in my inner room
playing my poetic permutations
can only look and ask the unanswerable.

Brave and cunning I speak to my typewriter
knowing it will not answer back
knowing it will not reply
what I ask and do not want to hear
as you with the vast sunset merge
a multitude of dreams away
uniquely alone and outside of me
in the purity and rarity of this moment
immeasurably beyond my love and my rage

and with the dying call of gulls
the echo resounds:

Girl in the wind
throwing aside
the tight shutters of my life –
which way are we going?

Finding

You touched my flawed body

                  so gently with your eyes
as later with the infinite gentleness

                  of your mind
when the world stopped screaming

               and turned to the slow rhythm
of our discovered music.

Improbably finding me out

            in that room reeking of smoke
and mindless bombast

            as islanded on the fringe of
frantic talk

            sourly aswim with whisky
lonelier than death

           and half in love with that grey
inevitability

        I counted my threadbare bag of pinched
blessings

        babbling in an idiot cell with no one
to hear my babytalk but myself

        till you came and sat beside me out of
nowhere

        utterly without preamble or verbal foreplay
as if only then we had come into existence

        out of some speechless experience
into where we then found ourselves

        talking our heads off and I remember
laughing a lot

        at and beyond ourselves

        dissecting Mr Joyce with gusto
discussing the myth-making antics of Yeats

        impetuously scaling his dark tower
and knowing behind the flying words

        new selves vastly unknown and unmet

before you entered that hellish room
on an everlasting instant of wonder.

Voices in a void droning on
bottle rotating from hand to flashing
hand
the bruised cloistered air throbbing with
the horror of lives spent
before they had begun
till another day new only to us
heaved itself over the rooftops
unseen behind moveless
curtains
though we had already left
had already travelled to where nothing could touch us
neither malice nor envy of word or eye
nothing concocted of gnarled minds
nothing remotely created could touch
us then
we a little in fright of what even then we already
knew
as the foolish brave unstoppable words poured
from us
even in the great and utter silence of our
hearts
telling us of the bright thing that had begun.

You touched my flawed life so gently with love
burning upward in dark steady flame
burning me, burning me into healing.

W. H. Auden

I came to you tardy and late
as I usually do to the better things in my life:
this hidden singing land I never knew
of eloquent weathers and the many-tongued sea
changing and ever changeless
drawing the moody skies into its mirror
and a true girl to love and steer my star by
at the comic end of it all
making me contemplate eternity
with rather less rash enthusiasm
than in my unspent years of dreaming.

Others kind in their way insisted I read you
as I climbed the slippery ladder out of my cosy accepted mire
and like being pressed with strong medicine I held back
recalcitrant as a surly upstart pup
growling in its soiled lair
snapping at the hands that would feed it.

You were dead before I stumbled upon the life that was in your
poetry
upending your generation and doing needful miracles
on the ones that came limping or thundering after;
dead but you would not lie safely down
and only in the final weeks did I see your face
televised out of human context
alien to that merciless medium
a craggy continent creviced with living
a rubbery sphere indented with tangled latitudes of honest pain
and the healing laughter that lies behind unambiguous suffering
speaking your verse in a tired unlit voice
as if you wanted to close the door and be gone
to where you might at last pin down peace
drink unending wine and converse with friends
till all the sacred cows came home

the ones that you had not so gaily slaughtered
on that mazed journey into truth.

I yet know only half of your mind
half of the world you made uniquely your own
and the other half beckons like an unexplored country
wherein I shall falter often early and late
be confused and befuddled by so many trails
lured by signs that lead apparently into nowhere
save that the nowhere you inhabited teemed with such life
as to leave me panting and many times lost
in my belated crusade to find you.

Love Song

Mary of ever morning light
enter as music into my waking

cover me with your tenderness
from the grey terrors of myself

yours the strength of flowers
rooted in crevices of my heart

out of the wanton wind's way
blossom in my darkness

bringing the laggard world alive
upon your smile and stilling

the night's rage and tumult
in wordless wealth of caring

deep as flowers or love can reach
your daily miracle of healing

Mary of ever morning light
always as music in my waking.

City Airs

When I was yet reaching to be a man
I met a quayside courtesan
with arrogant and immediate eyes
and no time for haggling compromise.

It was high July and in the shade
of the masted ships she plied her trade
and more for pity than quick silver pence
she taught me pain and commonsense.

She looked into my eyes and saw
the lineaments of leafy awe
and with deft sleight of hand and tongue
brought me the terror of being young.

With facile sleight of tongue and hand
she drew maps I did not understand
as the great ships with sails undone
lay festering in the squalid sun.

And in the surly conspiring shade
with lip and tongue and hand she played
hidden symphonies undefined
beyond the slipping grasp of mind.

With windswept hair from scarf unfurled
she held the rash wisdom of the world
taught me man's uniqueness from beast –
for one most singular hour at least.

Along the quays and into the flame
of sunset she went without a name
and my steps are back where it began
and still I reach out to be that man

who when his little hour had burned
got on a bus and never returned.

Act of Contrition

I am sad as the morning begins
for the sudden death of the simple life
I once imagined I was born for
lying deflowered now upon the tatty high altar of ambition
before it had a chance to enjoy its virginity.

Sad too in a remote metaphysical way
for the way things are in China;
reeking with rice and bamboo fervour
all that rice and all that fervour
all that murderous dedication
eternities of patient padded feet marching
pounding out miracles of anonymity
that universal good
choicest ruby in that stark crown
a vast sheet of carbon paper
drawn over the seething land
sucking the soul away.

I am sad for reading that stupid novel last night
wasting the nocturnal virtues of sea-watching
not remembering a single snide simper of it;
sadder still for writing that stupid novel last year
that shrill little Jericho of collapsible walls
throwing stones at myself
a stationary target
and not once hitting the mark;
in extravagant excess of contrition
I am already sorry for the novel I am about to write –
which is being sorry with a vengeance.

Today for want of somewhere else to exile my eyes
I watched the tide come in late
and felt sad for the laggard waves
lurching drunkenly on sharp-tongued rocks

like errant husbands belching home to fuming spouses
sure of a similar scalding;
the amatory cat slinking through the wet grass love-replete
belly touching ground in satiety
a drowned item the sea had disgorged
in disgust at its own gluttony.

Up in the dark saturnine Northland
studded with silent singsong lakes
and hills loud with dead men's tales
where once I heaped lavish untrue praises
upon a long-legged woman and lusted for her out of reason
until I put aside that curious little day
somebody is already being shot
for Christ and country
blood reddening the heather or pavement
the orange or green bullet
fired by us all awake or asleep
startling a leaf or window-latch with its report.

Most of all it saddens me to sit here
mooning like a calf besotted with afterbirth
and the abrupt dark draping the sky
writing lines like these so eminently qualified
to be contrite about.

Of Snails and Skylarks

He can tell the colours of the four winds
blowing over the rumpled rainbow land

pluck any miracle in or out of season
from out his patchwork bag of magic

slung over his starward-leaning shoulder
mad eyes playing tunes of enchantment

upon rock and leaf and curling grass
telling in the sere hedges of October

a thousand tangled themes and quirky tales
of canny snails and skylarks

He shakes the torpid earth awake
makes it throb beneath his hobnailed music

the smallest stream runs madcap at the sun
and fishes in tremulous depths conspire

to deliver up their sleek cunning
into his green-thumbed keeping

He holds converse with flowering stones
opening beneath his caressing feet

feasts upon bright philosophies of air
and leaving wraps his heart in a cloud

watches it smiling as it floats away
touching steeples as it goes

then laying aside his miracles and music
all wonder accomplished for another day

he forsakes the world of snails and skylarks
and steps sadly down into the harlot streets

that spawned and still sternly spurn him
hiding in his heart a smuggled fugitive joy

lighting the broad wasted dark of that meaner time.

Now and Not Then

Shall the dire day break when life
finds us merely husband and wife
with passion not so much denied
as neatly laundered and put aside
and the old joyous insistence
trimmed to placid coexistence?

Shall we sometime arise from bed
with not a carnal thought in our head
look at each other without surprise
out of wide awake uncandid eyes
touch and know no immediate urge
where all mysteries converge?

Speak for the sake of something to say
and now and then put on a display
of elaborate mimicry of the past to prove
that ritual reigns where once ruled love
and calmly observe those bleak rites
that once made splendour of our nights?

Dear, when we stop being outrageous
and no longer find contagious
the innumerable ecstasies we find
in rise of hand or leap of mind –
not now or then, love, need we fear thus;
those two sad people will not be *us*.

In Memory of Melba
Our Cat

You did not long enjoy
the unexplored wonders of this other Eden
you of the purring yellow-eyed persuasion
skipping in and so abruptly out of our lives
running rashly off into feline eternity
under the bouncing wheels of a country trailer.

No more than a kitten yourself, girl,
and we who had fumed at your early courting
are thankful now that you gave us as parting gift
three carbon copies of yourself as souvenirs
to help heal the wound of your passing
in a purring concourse of caring.

No more will you wake me from futile dreaming
your velvet presence padding over my face
miaowing me back to bleary-eyed reality
wanting not my meagre comfort
but to share your warmth with me
out of the sleek largesse of your nature.

The sea will be melancholy for a while
with you not there to distract me
from the due contemplation of beauty
by insisting that I look first upon your own
and for the first time in many weeks
the morning ashes will be undisturbed in the grate.

The new home that you had just begun to rule
will be loud now with your sudden absence
until the three gentle reminders you bequeathed us
begin slowly to fill the furry void.

Pique

My wife, otherwise an agreeable perspicacious helpmate,
has one pernicious failing:
she reads other writers.
A blatant act of infidelity
short of the other easier variety
which I could take in my stride
with a large pinch of arsenic.

She not merely reads other writers
but has the nerve to enjoy them
dissecting their outpourings
with critical élan
taking them to bed with her every night.
Not quite what the wife of a writer
ought really to do
when all is unsaid and undone
sending me into murky fits
of quite juvenile pique
as I take it out on my typewriter
belting it until its innards groan
banging my head against the invisible wall
of her insatiable booklore.

She spends hours away from me
locked in somebody else's world
embroiled in some other bloody writer's fantasies
quite ignoring the ones that are spinning round in my head
and despoiling innocent sheets of paper
as I eject them forth like spittle
not having anything better to do
between the cup and the leering lip.

A novel in her immaculate hands
becomes a desert between us
while I sourly contemplate

the alphabet on my keyboard
as between the literary covers she snuggles
shameless as sharing another bloke's bed.

What spectacle could be worse
than glowering impotent on the sidelines
while my wife devours with unappetised abandon
other traders of the word incarnate?

The Poetry Reading

Trapped and beleaguered in a web of guests
garrulous unto the perilous point of endurance
set upon ushering in the new day
with last-gasp wheezing of applause
we looked at each other
across the littered chasm of mashed cigarettes
and tumblers aswirl with debris of slaughtered drinks
looking for hopeful signs of departure
and as before found only gaping mouths
insatiable and unstoppable
opening on profligate inanities
bruising the reeking walls with ballads
patriotic paeans extolling the mercifully dead
roaring the praises of nubile native daughters
long removed from lascivious gaze
beguiling the worms with their mythic charms;
knee-thumping fists flailing in lickspittle emphasis
beating out our limp-lidded doom
sending the spectre of sleep scurrying
over the ink-black night bay
as gallant and gracious to the bilious end
we smiled and politely nodded and blinked our eyes
skewered to the convivial stake of friendship
hope of repose long kicked into exile
pacing the desolate hills
as the unending carousel continued
caught in a time-trap of bonhomie.

I slipped into threadbare refuge of apathy
listening with marginal focus of attention
as the court jester beside me told a joke
done to haggard death all evening
concerning a rural chiropodist
who, when asked to lend a hand to a stranded pub-bound
      motorist,
could only proffer a foot . . .

Out of fierce self-willed torpor I awoke
to see a small miracle taking place;
holding the slim volume of my poems in your hands
as if holding a fiery Book of Job
in an attitude of implacable Thespian command
you were declaiming forth my pallid verses
in your best Bernhardt tones of faith
a deft Delphic nymph of sleeklimbed bombast
throwing pearls of imperishable truth and profundity
upon the slack-jawed philistines gathered at your feet
a receding sea of stunned befuddled faces
whisky hands stayed stupefied in mid-air
by this silk-and-steel siren of Poesy majestic in their midst
making each of them in quick turn suddenly homesick
and hastening en masse to quit the holy temple . . .

Alone at last we smiled
and raised a final glass in tired triumph and homage
to that slender sesame of our deliverance
you still held like a scimitar in your hands
as the waves broke and brightened below us
and waking birds shook the grey hedges into life.

Victoria

From this unimagined pinnacle of my new life
every gentle now and then you come back
out of a past neither of us ever really knew
still less apprehended with total mind
save as sometimes we remember music
heard only in dream
and all the more real for that
touching chords buried beyond words to capture
beyond life's sad erosions.

I made for you once a small poem
born out of a comic cameo you had painted
of you working minor kinetic miracles
at some crazy pre-dawn California carnival
wherein I begged you not to look
too closely into my shopsoiled soul
and in mercy turn aside those merciless lenses
for fear you would finally discover me;
thankfully you looked the kinder way
sparing me at least that truth
that so graced your letters.

Your name fell exotic on my senses
hardened to plainer greyer sounds
and I recall how at last
after talkative eons of pages
had traversed the ocean between us
you brought to the surface of our dialogue
the particular pigmentation of your skin
long before the paltry pundits of popular idiom
had ever linked black with beautiful;
in turn you knew well enough by then
the many-weathered colours of my mind
to wonder about the hue of my skin.

You scared and shamed me with your young intensity
angry with the collective stupidities of humankind
making my zealous apathy a tawdry fake
my well-tended sophisticated boredom with life
a hollow laugh in an empty banquet hall
my heart a vessel looted of compassion.

Yesterday was something we savoured
with our finer perceptions
with keener felicities of sense
than are likely to attend us ever afterwards;
with the unreturnable rhythm of the sea
impassable and wide as destiny
yesterday ebbed away
found refuge on another safer shore
leaving fragile imprints
we shall trace in our minds forever.

Beached now under my singular star
lighting me into new understanding and love
you shine on the soft pure rim of that world
and enter ever gentle now and then
with gifts of simple peace and charity in your hands

making the broad spaces between us
flower with meaning.

Vamp

All jaded airs and faded graces
out of daylong hibernation you emerge
to saunter down the main street swivel-hipped
high heels clacking on cobblestones
beating out a staccato come-hither beat
mascaraed eyes alert for evening commerce
lashes dark and lustrous and not your own
lacquered hair piled in perilous pyramids
some incautious chap might in a soft moment touch
and pull fingers away stung as from barbed wire.

You are an anachronism and you know it
had you words to frame the thought
but are too tired to care
for the need that drives you down such mean ways
is never outdated.

Men with hunted rabbit faces
married past recollection of slighter freedoms
teetering with sick qualms into tepid middleage
ogle you in the gloom of the lounge bar
their brood hens of wives sipping gin and tonic
moistily enmeshed in home truths and grandchildren
and the automatic smile of response
cracking your rouged and powdered cheek
flutters a moment in the musty air
and falls to grief into the deep-pile carpet
midway between you and those stout agricultural wallets
stricken across a minefield of grassy boots
and sodden cigarette ends

and the faint Lotharios turn aside
smirking into their pints
settling for domestic twilight
and the naggin home in the hip pocket.

And nobody sees you home save the stars
and the mangy mongrel yapping at your ankles
frantic for want of a kind slurred word
out of your twisted red mouth.

Cursing you lunge into the wailing night
raw brambles tugging at your ancient fur jacket
lifting the jarring latch on your door
kicking out the world of tight pockets
and tighter mercies.

To the flickering grate you stumble
numbed hands outstretched
to catch the last of the heat
from the embers of the only fire left.

Lonely Madrigal

London flounders in my Lady's golden wake.

In this crabbed hour of lonely themes
cracked lads and freckled lasses of my stripling years
come crowding back to cloud the dusty mirror of memory
stirring dulled images of vanquished vanities
as that fabulous bringer of my latecoming joy
once more claims London as her own
and gathers it into her scented palm.

Risen from playful dust they return
to taunt my jaded genes with remembered verve
laughing dare-devil lads and scornful sun-licked girls
as stooped and bent with loss
I crouch above my typewriter
dredging murky depths for words to drown the image
of the morning star of my querulous middle-years
dangling London on the pellucid tips of her fingers.

In puny rage I populate this tumultuous silence
with hoarse affirmations of self-sufficiency
battling with elements attuned to inner mayhem
carving upon the rude rock of time a brief postscript
of diminishing pith and traitor wisdom
borrowed from sources I no longer have right or light to enter
and only this patient beast of purring metal answers back
shuddering under my insane bellowings
as scoundrel London swivels and rotates
upon a turn of my Lady's impeccable wrist.

I claw out hidden hieroglyphics of meaning
in the threatening swarm of this early dark
creeping like ink across the unquiet bay
touching my mind with dire intimations of coming terrors
146

and the shawl of rough desperate logic I wrap round me
grows hourly more threadbare
admitting the dreaded draught of her intolerable absence
who quenches the lurid lamps of London in her look.

I huddle in the hollow rock of no solace
seeking refuge in past pretensions of peace
turning over random stones of once radiant hue
and finding underneath the utter blight of promise
filling with decay of unfound purpose this soulless room
left a graveyard rank and desecrated
as the torpid pulse of London quickens to her merest gesture.

O London I damn and excoriate you
and call down upon you a thousand plagues
as you flounder in my Lady's golden wake.

Over The Sea to Leeds

Kindly I told myself – a guest in your midst –
that you were in a state of transition
between falling down and standing up
as my friends introduced me to you
on that early morning tour
a hurried get-together I grant you
and from my high perch
eagle-eyed on the seat of the van
the local vista was restricted

yet charity has its bounds
eyes were after all made to see
and sadly I saw you at your Sunday worst
making that first dismal morning after disembarkation
more of a grey burden with your encrusted scabs
and open weeping sores oozing urban putrefaction
mocking the far green magic of the hills
receding like a distant dream of Summer away from you
your chimneys scumming the skies

dowager buildings of once civic bloom
huddled together like battered old ladies
in dingy defeated camaraderie
children flitting like lively lice
through the scalded maze of your streets
Sabbatical factory smoke drawing a murky shawl
over your pockmarked pools of desolation
your awful incongruity uncharmed by age
untouched by faint stirrings of a former grace.

I beheld you thus exposed in all your shabby lineaments
and to my utmost chagrin felt tortuously at home.

Broken Rhythm

There I was
grunting in the grey wizened morning
crouched on the hard functional lavatory pot
straining valiantly to do nature's business
and making heavy weather of it
aspiring to put my mind onto higher things
in that cramped smelly fly-besotted cubicle

when over the saloon-like swinging halfdoor
like a bulbous red moon over a hedge
rose a round capped countryman's face
honest in its perplexity and concern
puckered up with childlike curiosity
wanting to know if I needed – of all things – a hand.

For a moment I was angry
at this bovine intrusion
into what was after all an intensely private affair
between my gaseous intractable innards and myself
but soon my unfriendly resentment gave way
to humorous resignation
thinking how absurd our strident insistence upon privacy
in this turgid chamberpot-flush of a life

for at least the face mooning over the halfdoor
was unblemished with mockery
full of brotherly care at my comical plight
though it played bloody havoc with my rhythm.

Terminal Thoughts

Death bores the life out of me.

It no longer intrigues or invites speculation.
It happens so often it has become monotonous.
It is an overplayed exercise in melancholy
akin to sex in its inflated reputation.

What offends me most about death
is its abject lack of imagination.
As often as not it is a dull business
denying that sense of theatre
immured in the dullest soul
seldom nudging us over into fantasy.

We seldom get the death we deserve.
As in life second-best is the reigning norm.
The vast grey majority of men and women
die deaths of unsurpassed mediocrity
bathed in a thin aura of pointless poignancy
giving us slight pause in our crowded trivia
to make clichéd comment upon the piquancy of the end.

In our urgency to liven it up a bit
we invest death with an inventive streak
it does not remotely begin to possess
except of course when it happens to us.
Then it is a sad and magnificent thing
compelling the respect and compassion of all who gaze upon it.
Then for the first time in our lives perhaps we hold the stage
and nothing is going to cheat us of the limelight
least of all the mundane act of dying.

Death is so often a distinct non-event.
Even the most incandescent of lives

can be ruined by a wretched curtain
falling halfway between a belch and a sigh.
And princes too once bluff and portly as Hal
of far-famed bestialities and resplendent lusts
seldom thunder topheavy into laughing graves
but choke to death of obese surfeit on a mouldy wine cork
and slide into ponderous boxes wormy with weariness
or lacking even that last lachrymose grace
linger like chilled refugees in the bleak deserted foyer
long after their insipid little drama is over
to splutter into infantile incoherence
on soggy sodden gobbets of gutless bravado
stuck in their wasted gullets.

Death and dignity seldom see eye to eye.
The best way to die is to be alive while you are doing it
with all five senses and others in full flight
in full-throated green-gold career
before the final obscenity of linen sheets
that unnatural landscape of dim candles and muted voices
and gloved hands pressing forth in observed ritual grief
lest we awaken in another time and overhear
these pallid lamentations hurting our repose
and weep for having once been alive.

Friend, you are more than welcome to death;
it is something I can well do without.

Lapwing

Lapwing alighting
bringing the morning alive
setting the sad sea in motion
putting the tardy sun in its place

making the grass leap before our eyes
dipping gracefully into our lives
taking earth and sky under wing
a quiver of sleek pride

then into the morning with you.

A Kind of Prayer

Call me, Lord, as call You must
in the carnival midst of my sins
for surely that is where it all begins
at last to make sense of this foolish dust
when the all too escapable charms
and infidel conspiring alarms
that hold us tightly in thrall
as we precariously crawl
about our little plot
loosen and lamely fall
from our inhospitable skins
and nothing more we crave
of sunset or dawn
prizes lost or newly won
or tenacious images haul
from our initial nowhere
above or below the indifferent air
within or beyond the garrulous grave
our brief bolt shot
with no need then to act brave
or lament our gaudy lot
and we no longer there.

Call me, Lord, as call You will
in the dawn or dusk of sinning
while I still dream of winning
one more rowdy hour to fill
my mouth full of the usual stuff
of nonsense and whisky in measure enough
to buoy me through another day
content to let the devil pay
my eyes peeled for sudden wonders
on every random breeze
still capable of self-surprise
and unwarrantable surmise

still adept at making blunders
in traversing the thin trapeze
above the torn nets of sanity
the waiting pitfalls of inanity
O I'd rather go while I am ahead
before having to pay the inevitable toll
with my inconsequential soul
against all debts accumulated
as I dawdled and procrastinated
in earning my daily bread –
bad enough at any time to be dead
without going on the immortal dole.

Come get me, Lord, awake or asleep
in prancing April or sad-eyed October
wild in my cups or ponderously sober
and if that most singular girl should weep
at whose footfall my aspirations leap
give her all the comfort You can
with promise of a happier plan
just waiting around the next bend –
let her know my passing isn't the end
of all brighter things to come to her
that light and music can still occur
with me no longer hanging around
to mutter a single possessive sound.

Come swift or slow, Lord, loud or soft
under swoon of moon or glare of day
with my crazed senses with me or away
bearing me downward or aloft
as long as You come where my story begins
in the merciful heyday midst of my sins.

John Millington Synge

Uncouth as the wind
rising out of mist and fire
you heeded as the sea told tales
and yielded up to you its passionate lore.

Transfixed by rainbows you stood
by the gaping wounds of the smitten land
and emptied your painful soft-vowelled love
into its bitter dreaming brood.

Let wiser minds than I possess
grant or deny your place as seer and singer
of blood themes more wildly imagined
and still more savagely lived
now passed from the tongues of men
beyond pale logic to discover or dissect
for having once lived in or out of time
beauty lives forever shadowed in its own radiance.

I only know you brought the roar of Aran waves
crashing in angry splendour upon my stony threshold
and caused the walls of my bleak solitary room
to blaze brightly once with heather and thistledown

hurting my city-snared eyes
and troubling my heart out of muteness
until sparrow and skylark were one
bearing the rooftops away.

Lost Item

The man was crying
                        as no child could ever cry
hard bitter wailing
                        unforced as raw act of nature
shaking his birdcage chest
                        draped in ignominious hospital pyjamas
stooped in wan morning light by high-barred window
                        vein-curdled hands clasped
rigid as taut-strung wire
                        tonsured head bowed in bereavement
as the day rattled and clattered
                        cups passed around
swimming with tepid tea.

Male nurses in brisk no-nonsense white uniforms
                        whom I had maligned as "deflowered eunuchs"
the night of my admittance
                        twisting in whisky fulminations
were ordinary blokes again doing a job
                        shaking out night-rumpled sheets
turning man-soiled mattresses
                        spoon-feeding infirm tremulous men
whose ages could no longer be deciphered
                        lost in rambling mazes of oblivion
swift adept young hands wiping dribbling drooling mouths
                        tender as any woman and companionable
exchanging ribald anecdotes of nights off
                        whistling the latest pop tunes
taking no notice whatever
                        of the weeping man.

Red-eyed and hating the world
                        I peered over the rough rim of my blanket
wincing at the din of delf
                        the clang and canker of morning

creeping out of my bestiary of bludgeoned pleasures
                                beholding the man then crying in light
amazed by such unchecked male grief
                                wondering how these cheery young men
uniformed in the business of healing
                                could bear to pass him by unheeding
standing by the cell-like window
                                blighted by some unnameable loss
tears making mockery of his harpooned manhood
                                swaying barefoot on cold boards
a thin blue-striped totem pole
                                uprooted and left to brutish elements
riven down his scarecrow lacerated length.

Unable further to stand the spectacle
                                easily outraged by bland faces
passing unobservant and incurious all about
                                in loud hearty ups-a-daisy bonhomie
I demanded a key to this sorrowful mystery in our midst
                                and was informed by a brash young scallion
of under twenty amid a white welter of teeth:
"Michael Joe, is it?
                        Oh, he's a bit upset
because he can't remember where
                                he left his fuckin' dentures last night –"
He paused square hand assured in mid-air
                                and smiled winningly down –
"It *is* two spoonfuls, isn't it?"

Cobra

Habit
coiling uncoiling
cobra in grass
strangling strong and delicate
strands of ancient affinities
poison drawing poison
minus hope of antidote
save the slippery slide
home into oblivion
the dying unending
and that too an illusion
windowless reality
mirroring always
the threat of tomorrow
deadlier than bite of now
oozing into pores
liquefied terror
slithering
cobra in grass.

Antiseptic den
of shambling shadow men
coughing up life
uniformed in despair
chained ankles rubbing
the cobra waits
coils uncoils
moves slow
slinky with intent
forking fangs
into sodden minds
soft as rotten fruit
gargoyle charade
brainless unison
invisibly fettered

life once shared
once consummated
shredded
sick moist joke
dribbling into apathy
slackjawed
in the final reel.

Habit
viperish wise
slicing
through caring
killing roots
no more indomitable
once strong
as love called home
redemption
cold echo
in wilderness
little shambling mice-men
twittering in a cage
biting
the quick of their lives
in swift savage snaps
gleeful in dying.

Habit
is what I wear now
snug as the last shroud.

Morning Glory

Above the morning waves I behold
in a tumble of brown and gold
my Venus rising from the sea –
albeit somewhat listlessly.

The enchantment of the waking shore
cannot quite banish the night before
as with hair in glorious disarray
she stumbles forth to greet the day.

Over the coffee and untouched toast
I see traces of last night's ghost
lurking in those fabulous eyes
unwilling to meet the breaking skies.

Lo, the sun ignites her hair, and she
turns that radiant look on me
and with breathless intonations
murmurs of perilous palpitations.

Light and delight of eye and limb
moving as one inspiring hymn
weaving with lithe deliberate tread
her precarious way back to bed.

Leaving me to contemplate
in my own somewhat unsteady state
how even Beauty of such queenly shine
cannot quite outwit a little wine.

Dear Dilemma

This is surely the ultimate catalyst –
you are off to see your analyst.

The ageless story reads so well –
less now of heaven and more of hell;
you no longer derive stimulation
from my brilliant conversation;
as I pulsate with volcanic desire
you sit reading novels by the fire
your mind elsewhere to strangers grown
and not one of the bloody novels my own;
not only do you shun my perennial company –
you don't even glance now at my latest poetry
a fate that is infinitely worse than death
for one who spews verse with every breath.

Where once my witticisms would have scored
now they merely make you bored
and those outpourings you once deemed lyrical
now only render you slightly hysterical
for try as you might you cannot disguise
the desperation in your eyes
the peculiar way you hold the breadknife
while I babble on about the sanctity of life
as from heights we once considered exotic
I bring you down to the merely neurotic.

Most evenings now we sit glassy-eyed
every small tension magnified
warding off mutual scorn and derision
staring blind and mute at television
all past delights gone sour and cloyed
as you get ready at length to meet your new-found Freud
leaving me alone to wince and contemplate
the bare brittle bones of our marital state

neither lovable clown nor nimble sage
sinking too soon into bilious middleage.

You married me for better or for worse –
but you reckoned without my atrocious verse
or the times I would limp from my mental hovel
to have another tired go at that damn novel
the English of Avon's Swan to bludgeon
with apoplectic flights of pith and high dudgeon
hammerstrokes of bucolic grit and wrath
slithering down the traitorous path
of inordinate imagined wrongs and indignation
with notions immeasurably above my station
which far from making you proud or elated
made you gradually quite sedated.

And in your eyes there sometimes hovers
shades of past innumerable lovers
who would grovel for your merest touch
and count themselves blessed if you as much
as brushed their hapless brows with your lips
sending them spinning over into total eclipse
hastening to your every beck and call
poor slaves and besotted servants all
cast aside desolate and discarded
disconsolate and broken-hearted
floundering in your starry wake
all for my bombastic sake.

And this is the melancholy final twist
beyond cure by faith quack or psychiatrist;
hellfire in my breast will continue to rankle
as my life story twines around your delectable ankle.

Dolphins

Out of dreamy early morning eyes we saw them
rising upon the languid incoming waves
disporting themselves with impish grace in the sun
as if gliding that bright moment out of fantasy
solely for our shared unutterable delight.

Pearly portents of promise in the infant day
forging a private ballet for our waking eyes
indifferent to our silent applause
giving us brief entrance
to their lucid universe.

Making us pause to marvel at the music
in slow stir of surf and sigh of leaf
lending to our minds gentle assurance
of sharing with these shining friends
our little clifftop eyrie of heartsong.

In the instant it took our entranced eyes
to lift and find each other again
they had gone back into fantasy
lest we suffer by our gazing
too great a surfeit of joy.

They danced upon the waves long afterwards
a wineglow upon our gladdened senses.

A Song For My Body

What quite undivine act of comedy
landed us together in the same suit of skin?
Welded as one in this ungainly unholy alliance
so often with damn all to say to each other
communications awry and in a tangled mess
of jangled nerve-endings that never end
transmitting like drunken telephonists
bawling out contradictions in beleaguered defiance
wading through a morass of perennial cross-purposes
screaming frenzied morse code signals
when there is no marrow of meaning in the messages?

Sing a song of no pence
retrogressive nonsense;
what sort of clown is at the helm
of our incongruous realm?

Thrown into this crazy unending waltz
without preamble or introduction
without being asked if we even liked one another
we trip each other up at every hazardous step
stumbling over cunningly concealed obstacles
locked in a sweaty unwelcome embrace
in a twist of unaesthetic turbulence
in a murderous shadow-game of coexistence.

A rare time the miracle happens;
freedom's bright brief shaft falls between us
as out of orbit we dance in our separate spheres
only to collide once more in explosive conjunction
come as ever too soon upon the old weary reckoning
and crawl again inside the same hateful habitation
skulking and seething in our mutual loathing.

164

Sing a song of no hope
for poor derided joe soap;
what mocking hand pulls the string
of our inelegant capering?

In the narrowness of your lean miserly means
I splutter like a guttered candle
taunted by the tantrums of your absurd cravings
your flashing prima donna swoops of need
the gold and grey of your solitudes and solstices
as groaning you heave yourself over the brow of another day
the hard hours contracting to points of no meaning
as you square up to them with tired tinselled bravado
peering through the faded plumage of your dusty decades
and even as I call to you in baffled tenderness
and fury in the ceaseless fray
you lag forever a million heavy years behind.

Sing a song of alien rye
to hell with the wherefore and the why;
what master magician all logic defying
 oins us in this long lugubrious dying?

And still there was a summer . . .
the hot easy contempt of a greener time
stretched at weary length into disgruntled afternoon compromise
after many a false clarion call of passion and alarm
when the blood bounded between us like a sea in torment
love came for the once and only time and made you eloquent
made you almost unique and beautiful
unafraid to acknowledge the presence of mirrors in the world
made of our mutual cell a strange sanctuary
made you weep for the new singing that was in you.

Sing a song of hands and feet
see how the bruised lovers bleat;
what supreme satirist calls the tune
and hails us home from the fair too soon?

When we have been served the last taste of living
and the landlord bellows Time for the last time
I hope we can be gentlemen, you and I, and quietly take our
    leave
with no hangdog regrets or malingering back after hours
when there is nothing left in the bottle but the dregs of yesterday
and you slip into the final folly of the grave
bones and sinews no longer at the beck of random voices
your empty passages strumming with industrious worms
and that daft bewildered battery-box of a brain
all loose screws and twisted wires brittle like wintry twigs
settles into its unfamiliar quietude –

We face another puzzle:

When the crying's over and the quick tears dry –
who will have the last laugh, you or I?

Memo to a Fellow Sufferer

Where do you ride tonight, brother bard,
upon the range under the stars?
Chatting up the mots of Madrid
bedazzling the birds of Barcelona
with that liquorice tongue of yours
meddling with their mantillas
under dark Moorish walls
so many alien Mollies blooming
where the sperm flows as fast as the brandy?

Do you perchance sit and sup
with fanatic thin-lipped jesuits
plotting the come-uppance of the state
your full May moon face shining
with prospects of arcane anarchy?
Still persecuted by Liffey nightmares
still fat and foolish as a fox on booze and bombast?
In your sensuous siestas do you sometimes catch
the slap of Arklow waves turgid
against barnacle-thick painted hulls?
Above the roar of the bullfight
the dying bellow of the bull
do you sometimes hear the far screech of Moore Street
the beloved fishwives of fable belting your ears?

You're not missing much
so slay the illusion of nostalgia
before it gets you in its tentacles again.

The Hail Marys are thick in Dublin tonight
and there's another bloody penny on the pint.

Nocturnal

Across the sleeping bay
a yellow moon plays havoc
with the cloudy continents
throwing a truculent charm
over shape and form and shadow
alive in coiled suspension
piercing the smooth thin shell
trapping capricious thought.

Symphonic waves below
shed dark pulses of peace
on the craggy foreshore
stark fingers reaching
in arrogant moonlight
hurting with jagged hints
of simple witchcraft
creeping about the murmuring room.

Gradual joy breaks
surging upon slow waves
glints of bruised brilliance
breaking upon brittle barriers
routing tired old suspicions
a silver shoal to read magic by
and lost shipwrecked things.

Faces from another time
articulate with love
rise between the moon and tears
unbidden from a buried somewhere
blind the white world of sea and cloud
for a long glimmering moment.

The Dunce

I could certainly live without you if I tried;
it is the trying that is so unthinkable.

I could learn to live alone with myself again
if I was not such a poor scholar at learning
that kind of intricate monumental lesson
and be able to go back into the cave again
and find my steps in the once familiar dark.

I could, for instance, watch a sunset without you,
hear birds without wishing to share their song with you,
listen to Mahler or Sibelius of a single evening
and not rage to have you in the same room.

The sea would surely speak the same things to my mind
and deliver up its immemorial magic as ever
with you not there to decipher it for me
with magic the sea could never own.

In your absence I might even write a love poem
and afterwards read it to the listening night
without choking to death on the mangled words
and losing all sense in the grief of your going.

I could find my way into books again without you
maybe into the writing of books without you
and not know the terrifying panic and sweat
of showing you what I have written.

I could begin to understand the hieroglyphics of my life
without you there to decode each symbol for me;
the little mysteries might unravel themselves
without your tender tutelage to prepare me.

Learning to live without you would be rather like
learning to die each moment I drew breath
and if that is the most vital lesson I can learn
let me remain a dunce the rest of my days.

Moon Ruse

They were lovers
of an ordinary stamp
and did not see flowers
other than things in a field
heard music as pleasant sounds
coming out of instruments
holding no ecstatic terrors
bringing no holy unease
to their mild middling minds
and when they held hands
no fire flashed between them
no symphony of panic swelled
crashing as the sea in giant need
and they looked at each other kindly
without being thunderstruck
the blood in their veins easeful as pipesmoke
and found life good.

Until the conjuring moon
one night told them lies
weaved fantasies of unbelief
till flowers were fables of glory
music a torrent in the air
rending the clouds with fire
the very stones underfoot
high altars of desire unfathomed
leading into abysses of surpassing joy
hung jewel-like upon their fingertips
the blood in their veins raging as Lucifer
calling up fiery kingdoms of sense
drowning in swoons of discovery
making life a livid word made flesh.

In the morning mild and married
they ask politely did the other sleep well

pass the marmalade and milk
spoon their tea dreamily
and contemplate the potted plants
lying on the windowsill
before the clock tells them
they are once more released
into their separate day.

The moon merely informs them now it is time for bed.

Remembering A Friend:
Robert Collis

The horse came back alone
over the morning hills of Wicklow
no longer bearing its master
missing the gentle guidance of your hand
nudging it into homecoming
mistily wondering perhaps
why you had stayed behind
why you had fallen
so soft and sudden
to earth
wordless in the wet grass
a moment ago you had ridden over like the wind
surveying your green valley as ever with love.

Down that smoking air a lone calling
hushing your high heart in a cloud
bearing you away from the valley and the city
from tenements darkly swarming with stunted life
and sibilant streams and hedges brimming with song
you knew and celebrated with conjoined agony and affection
that sudden swift whisper on the wind
in one swallow rush of zealous possession
stealing your breath past stream and pavement
in that moment out of time
that finds each of us small and alone
though wind and rain and growing things of earth
were brothers to you in that last union
and sang you proud into peace
under a turbulent sky
where your heart's abiding passion lay.

You strode rather than stepped through life
crushing many a demure bloom in your career

yet with the blunt sensitivity of one
trading not with images but imperatives
you were solicitous of mute mayhem
crashing through lives indignant with healing
the arrows of your anger flashing into minds
cramped and closeted in grey contumely of office
physician to the anonymous poor and maimed
loud with tenderness for broken things
making strength and basilicas of belief
out of the deep unsaid sorrows of your life
vain and strong and innocent of malice
and beautiful in the last and only sense.

Friend of all my life
seer of my sapling years
I do not feel your absence as pain
for knowledge of love once gained and given
is never lost or betrayed into unknowing
and there are always rainbows.

Men At Work

They loomed out of a grey nowhere
monkey-jacketed against the wind and sly rain
leaning on their trusty shovels chewing philosophies
cupping gutted cigarettes in knuckly fists
no doubt weighing things of high import
between their leather boots and the hanging skies
making the highways safe for cosseted citizens like us
passing by cocooned in cushiony warmth
while they the warrior workers
stood stoic sentinel
spades at the ready
opening up the country for commerce.

At our approach they became workmen once more
making heroic stabs at the wet unyielding tarmac
digging diligently into the hard business of the day
making ingenious little holes in the road
fussy as old maids at pastry
watching us out of hooded wary eyes
as we sped on through the mud
leaving them in the mist
to their butt-ends and craggy ponderings.

We thought it no small deed in our honour
that they had enterprise enough
to at least fake industry
stirred by flurries of decent guilt
while in paper-barricaded citadels across the land
the sleeping masters of the stately ship
stretched dishonourable limbs
and whistled in their subsidised slumbers
waking up between snore and avaricious fantasies
to exhort the populace anew
to greater frenzies of sacrifice
and national fervour.

A Handful of Haiku

1   *Dylan Thomas*
        Out of dawn raging
                in shoals of fire by the sea
      and bile-green bottles.

2   *Jonathan Swift*
        The demented dean
                stabs his quick quill on parchment
      to Vanessa's heart.

3   *Polonius*
        Behind an arras
                dispatched with a Danish thrust
      a paternal spy.

4   *Quasimodo*
        A lump of foolish flesh
            slobbering forth your rage and
                    fiercer farce of love.

5   *Sean*
        Ambition unlit
                poor as Christ in Bayswater
      your heart's your coffer.

6   *Dubliner*
        Raw rock-blasting voice
            anointed with Liffey dew
      woos a Spanish maid.

7   *At Two Years Old*
        My nephew runs in
            despoils my easel gaily
                puts Pablo to shame.

8   *That Cat*

Yellow evil-eyed
purrs through my leonine wrath
and licks my distaste.

Back At Base

The bruised air roars.

I know somewhere out there
beyond the dense green curtains
there is quietness and pause
the beginnings of peace perhaps
in some little back pocket of this city
unmolested by restless minds
attuned to the bedlam
the ceaseless furore
the merciless mass of mechanised living;
but the illusion escapes me now.

Once in the midst of chaos
this moment almost beyond recollection
I could imagine peace
could conjure up images of tranquillity
in the lift and closing of an eyelid
and make it last long enough to forge a dream.

Now only the noise exists
only that is real
where once I bled life
and imagined all my weathers to be.

My nerve-ends terminate here
are beaten into atrophy
bludgeoned to stupefied abstraction.
Not even in fractured sleep
can I grasp the torn threads
leading back into illusion.

Who is dead –
this city or I?

Whose is the corpse I see before me
stretched rigid in the comic contours of death –
my own or those streets that once rejoiced
in the dark and pearly time of my ascending hours?

The answer is not here
but elsewhere in a maze beyond unravelling.

I will come back to this place
again and ever again
and not ever find it again
for not even as a ghost am I at one with it.

Where once song sprang out of cement
and birds regal in stone
now only cement remains
and it no longer speaks bright talk to my mind.

Unearned Income

I have wrestled with death
of a kind
fought the dreary fight
a solo for two voices
in a minor key
one strident with fishwife imperatives
my own a slurred belch
heaved upon a mountain of monotony
upon which I have built my temple
squarely in quicksand.

A jejune joust with death
a tame contest
the outcome assured
in an arena swarming with dusty echoes
and still more dusty choices
in undistinguished darkness
with nothing solid underfoot
nothing palpable to assail
rend apart with absence of logic
hammer into shapelessness.
A boring battle of dull intent
without spectators
without clamour
utterly without glory
the bronzed bedlam of trumpets
no lurid thirst after victory
nor the greater lust after defeat
holding only at its nerveless core
a tepid scepticism
cancelling out belief
in one's instinct to survive
rendering the gilt-edged triumph
of the ageless adversary
a timeless static mockery
trapped in cold laughter.

So have I succeeded
in the crooked middleways of my fourth decade
to this score of unearned income
of sour sedentary wisdom
curled in upon itself
suckled on morbidity
limply taking my own pulse
noting its nonrate
zooming to cosmic zeros of indifference
as the sun climbs bravely out of torpor
to begin another round of weary salutation
on limbs vilely sprawled in acquiescence
and eyelids fast shut against intrusions of joy.

If such be the sum of worldly wisdom
life is then an impoverished joke
and death too great an anti-climax
to warrant serious attention
a hesitant kick in the teeth
where there are only soft gums left.

Beloved Myth

Behold the staunch suburban poet –
though his lines don't always show it –
enduring with grim-jawed tenacity
the trials of his trim-lawned Gethsemane
the heartscald of that promiscuous jade
practitioner of the poetical trade
striving to make his oracle heard
above the hissing of the absurd
looking on the masses with sardonic smile
inviolate in his inner self-exile
bidding loutish latter-day Horsemen pass by
with cold satirical and bloodshot eye
doing daily battle with the mental life
trying to forget he has a wife
padding about downstairs in curlers and slippers
endlessly embroiled in baked beans and kippers
as he meanwhile fumes and waits for the Holy Ghost
up there in his lonely observation post
a garret by chance carpeted and centrally heated
ensconced in armchair with pipe and pouch seated
the Sensitive Planted so beloved of Shelley
scaling Parnassus on well-nourished belly
with aesthetic energies to spend and burn
reaching at Fate's every barbarous turn
for bare bodkin or draught of swift hemlock
and finding the Jack Daniels still in stock.

Haunted hypochondriac and scholarly rake
steeped in the rustic lore of Clare and Blake
again excavating those satanic mills
in quest of metaphysical thrills
tireless indomitable intrepid wordsmith
daily living his secret beloved myth
that alone makes his life endurable
and his sanity almost insurable

preferring those Dantesque abysses
to the prattlings of the missus
that nymph of kippers and baked beans
slouching through Arcady in scruffy jeans
bringing him ham rolls and chicken soup
ministering to the marauding troop
of merest gut-need and appetite
unaware of his poetic pain and plight
poor painted heavy-hoofed Diana of the kitchen
mouthing endearments quite unbewitching
unknowing object of his private derision
oscillating between radio and television
blithe and trite and blissfully unheeding
as over typewriter her Percy Bysshe lies bleeding
thrashing in throes of latest ode or sonnet
pinning his transcendental soul upon it
while in the steamy nether regions downstairs
his lass of the most indelicate airs
lights up her umpteenth fag of that morning
and screams several shrill octaves without warning
for him to come down and show his husbandly mettle
by fixing the bloody plug on her electric kettle . . .

O though the world may never know it
he is every seedy inch a poet
as in clouds of fancy he sits alone
hugging the soul he thinks is his own.

Past Portrait

I sat for my friend the artist during a dull week
daring him to find me with his deft chalky strokes
drinking straight vodka and jabbering bright rubbish
never guessing he would unearth what he did
discover that which lay gnarled and hidden
beneath elaborate mounds of mimicry
and nudge it into such livid truth
no mirror could ever give back
finally leaving me wordless though glaring
confronting a stranger I knew darkly well
and wished not ever to know in light
vodka no longer victorious over visions
dredged up from depths I thought invulnerable
down years of diligent burial of things
that hindered cosy fantasies of self
held in a hollow shrine of careful conceit.

Yet there was fire then
the beginning of a voyage
anchored in proud solitudes
a surly arrogance almost noble
looking out at the woeful mess of a world
as if it owed me all the missing lore of life
and I would storm right out of time and claim it.

Four years on I stare at the face
a stranger I know not now in light or dark
and can discern but cannot feel the fire
nor remember the route of the journey
that floundered midway to nowhere
betrayed by an accident of truth.

Morning Song

Morning is where you move.

The strengthening sun
strokes the languid waves
gulls in a lazy ballet
perform miracles in still air
no longer wailing with necd
as if they too were replete
with promise lyrical on the wind.

Islands half hid in mist
move soft against the sky
smoke upon burnt glass
mountains conversing with clouds
too early in their splendour to intimidate
with familiar awe of alien homecoming.

I grope about for words
to capture the morning
as a bird in song on a clifftop branch
reminds me of my puny arrogance
with no note of mockery in its voice
knowing the true artist between us.

Without need of words
aureoling my world
you smile at my frantic pace
to express the inexpressible
harbouring my small despairs
keeping me new for wonder
cradling my song.

Morning is where you move
and love-lucid my senses follow.

Constancy

The shadow lingers
of our separate yesterdays
blurring with menace our present light
casting the false aura of other ancient ardours
between the bright tenacious passion that binds us
unbreakable now and for the unguessable future.

There are no more subtle ways I can speak to you
save in halting verse like now
begging your charity.

Often lost with futile freedom in a wilderness
or more stranded still with frailer freedom in a cage;
this then is our latter-day choice.

More remote than star is from star
likewise are we sometimes in a room
each captive of our ghosts
stretching silences once treasured
beyond the faint felicity of touch
a cold place between us
no words can fill.

Hope and great danger hover
in our merest response
yet however tenuous our tomorrow
the truth remains:
Love is by far
more constant than lovers are.

Between the uncertainty and the dream
persists always the possibility of failure;
between the hopeless tenderness
and the unutterable dread
the knife-twist of rational resignation
to what neither of us condones in the other.

Our every day burgeons with promise or threat
still between the endearment and the curse
Love remains by far
more constant than lovers are.

The shadow lingers
blunting our clearer perceptions
of the true and lasting in each other
making all the more foredoomed the escape
into lucid articulate latitudes
in either wilderness or cage.

And more than a shadow's journey from the other
is immensely more than we can contemplate
since Love remains by far
more constant than lovers are.

Hope and a gradual peace
to inform our understanding
is my prayer for the unreadable future;
the better times are not easily put aside
and the underrated things in our life
speak with greater gentler command
than passing wrath.

We lose each other in ways wilful and insignificant
yet Love remains by far
more constant than ever lovers are.

Sour Note On A Sweet Ending

When I yield to the ultimate folly and die
– O in the vast unforeseeable by-and-by! –
promise me dearest you will send
no plastic roses at the end
shed no inordinate tears
nor harbour any nagging fears
that after I am safely gone
I will desecrate your dawn
with ghostly disquiet or confusion
to shatter your fond illusion
that you really are quite free of me
for the rest of your mortality.

In death as never once in life
as safe remove from temporal strife
as if good breeding with the worms began
I shall become quite the gentleman
and like an ever perfect host
preserve you from my inquisitive ghost
and from that unseemly flood of language
that had caused you such dire earthly anguish
and surely you will smile to see
how solicitous and pleasant I can be
how uncommonly courteous and brave
from the unquerulous side of the grave
though you will perhaps brush tear from eye
and aspirate a wondering sigh
that such a weight of words should be
gone clean into the earth with me
with barely a tremor left behind
to aggravate your unmarried mind –
hardly more than a publisher's blurb
to vexate and momentarily perturb
the new-found rhythm of your days
and you at length free of my boorish ways

a philosophical drink by your side
alone in the companionable eventide
with me not there to plunder your peace
with unstoppable garbage without cease
while silently suffering you lift glass or cup
and mutely implore me to belt bloody up . . .

Ah dearest heart if you will but wait
I'll become the ideal soulmate
nevermore causing you a moment's trouble
and I but a mere ectoplasmic bubble
swaying above your gorgeous head
gruff and garrulous and safely dead.

A Blunt Instrument

Is my muse
a wild boar blundering blind
through delicate stems of themes
leaving a gory mess of butchered images
in its plundering wilful wake?

Maddened by murderous interior music
it ravages sunsets
captured once only by Turner
smears dark slivers of blood
across the face of the clearest moon;
the serenest swan static in majesty
upon evening waters
recoils from it in panic
and singing birds at its approach
drop like stones down the sky.

A thing of remorseless gluttony
of immense invincible vacuity
is my muse.

Yet it sang once in a rare moment
a small pure indomitable sound
escaping from twisted strings
and somehow after that
I could almost love the grotesque creature
as one can sometimes come to love the misbegotten.

Billy Nowhere

In smaller kinder places
where tongues are slow to taunt
and minds keep pace with turning leaves
he would have been acclaimed the village idiot
crowned with spiky laurels of honest wit and no malice
as something peculiar unto the wind
a few slates missing upstairs to be sure
but harmless and daft as a jackrabbit
dodging a friendly fusillade of potshots
aimed only to make him jump and never to maim.

In our deadlier clime no such mercies abounded.

We called him Billy Nowhere
for nowhere he seemed to be going
save up and down the murderous maze of roads
sweeping up the endless debris of other people's lives
falling into sudden profound reveries in the midst of dust.

O jealous we were of this readymade Quasimodo
streetcorner Caesars spawned in sewer depths of intent
hissing forth precocious maledictions to outwit serpents
aroused to young green bile by his intolerable innocence
jerking to the ragged rhythm of our spiteful mocking bells
clanging after him as he swept up rivulets of filth
banning him from our games of cocksure daring
forever devising new schemes of pointless pain
to rub his twisted nose in the gutters
the City Fathers hired him to clean
in all his twenty-very-odd years
of bovine boyhood enraging us
pale eggshell eyes puzzled
and a weak cunning grin opening to our queries
as we asked him what colour knickers
his sister wore at her shotgun wedding

and "None!" he cannily replied
knowing it would please us.

Leaning on his massive yardbrush in the watery morning
dustclouds gathering about his splayed hobnailed feet
his few thoughts creeping up and down his face
timid as mice uncertain of the light
trying to make out the mystery of our malice
sighing and wetting his horned hands with a manly spit
the better to get on with his streetcleaning destiny
shuffling off into the ineffectual sunset
his oxen hours nearing tired finale.

Later when he grew less "simple"
he would cadge pints off us in smoky bars
jabbering out the latest pop tunes
in a brownish spray of saliva
slobbering like a dog promised goodies
fawning upon our grownup snarled obscenities
the abbreviated ancient weekend suit hanging on his bones
in ragged parody of staunch hardihood
and at our braggart prompting he would follow
married women home at closing time
as far as their lighted windows
before flinging himself with manic glee
into the dewy midnight bushes above their shrill curses.

For all I know of him now in my crabbed nowhere decades
he is still sweeping the same blind streets
hounded by new hordes of devil children
his wrinkled monkey face dusty and undefeated.

Lost Lullaby

Where oh where has my innocence gone
where oh where can it be?
I mislaid it some years ago I recall
in a house of cheap love on the quay.

Where oh where has my innocence gone
where oh where can it be?
It dissolved in tears of petty rage
when the world refused to praise me.

Where oh where has my innocence gone
where oh where can it be?
It fled when the friend I trusted most
played the fool and began to trust me.

Where oh where has my innocence gone
where oh where can it be?
I lost it the day my heart became wise
and refused to return to me.

My innocence fled and took away
the key to my prison soul
leaving no star to falter by
and no crumbs for my beggar bowl.

It will not come back again
however my promise beguiled
until the man forgets his foolish estate
and greets the world as a child.

Oriental

How sad
To be alone in Taipeh
sipping Rose's lime juice
knowing your favourite lotus flower
lies tonight with a lesser envoy
from a country not mentioned
in the best circles.
Thinking how the coming nights
will be so many dyspeptic yawns without her,
recalling as you clean your teeth
the tumult of her sapling thighs
catapulting you into heavens beyond count
recalling her soft giggling vowels
against your stifled mouth
in the month of the long moon
in the cool white room of remote charm
facing China.

How sad
standing on the filthy railway station
brown briefcase in hand
pig eyes lost behind thick lenses
waving farewell to your boss the ambassador
who that night will resume undiplomatic relations
with his wife of the varicose-veined legs
and daunting Everest bosom;
thoughts snap at you like gnats
provoking a mild despair
and quietly you cry into yourself
recalling the empty room back at the embassy
her imprint everywhere, the sheets and pillows,
the Axminster carpet, in the scented bathroom
airy with lotus blossoms climbing the walls.
Tonight there will be no sleep in the room facing China,
thinking of her crushed like silk

under the lesser envoy;
perhaps you will then at last think of your wife
back home in bed in Westchester County
state of New York
snuggling down with caramels and Steinbeck.

How sad
alone in Taipeh
sipping Rose's lime juice
waiting to go mad
hearing the mocking laughter begin
of hidden perfumed harlots who will taunt without let
in the dog-eaten months of the long and short moon
facing China.

Slug Song

Consider the ubiquitous slug
be it snail, termite or bug
asking nothing save stalk or leaf
quite untroubled by metaphysic belief
inhabiting palaces of rock and river
sliding through life with sinuous quiver
minute lord of the plenteous earth
devouring it for all its diluvial worth.

By man's inveterate wrath subjected
to man's vast follies it stays unaffected
and I note yet another instance of its sagacity
wriggling along with such admirable tenacity;
however long it may have dawdled and tarried
I have yet to hear of a slug getting married
while I sit surrounded by manifold reminders
of what should have been eye-opening blinders
of what man's foolhardy supercilious estate
has wreaked on that most singular state
as I sadly contemplate my own crass contributions
to that enriching pluperfect of institutions.

And O joyous excellence of the humble slug –
it meanders through time without need of drug
crawling with sedate resolve to its destiny
undulating with serpentine zest and assiduity
and what matter if it fails to deduct or think –
certain it is that the slug does not drink
for who ever heard of bug, termite or worm
no matter how madly they shiver and squirm
in all manner of primordial esoteric dances
going into silly transcendental trances?

O how I envy snail, termite and slug
snug as God willed it in the proverbial rug
all petty guile lacking and unassuming
never once knowing what it is to be human.

A Question For Myself

Letters of hangdog devotion
moist with fatuous nostalgia
trickling in from your past
every other month or so
from a person now stateless in your realm

strike me as both ridiculous and sad
as though watching a cripple on crutches
buoyed up by invincible optimism
trying to cross a crowded thoroughfare
to catch the last bus
that left ages ago.

It's a form of obscenity
this burrowing back into the past
such ardent archaeology of dead stones
never letting the relics abide in peace
never allowing the past to be decently dead.

I too am invincible in my optimism
cocksure you won't throw him a spar
or help him across the busy street
that now like a vast prayer divides you
cocooned in my snug assurance
knowing it is with me you'll be watching
the rise and fall of every new and old moon
from this blessed day on to the inconceivable end.

Round every corner of mind and eye
you are there to startle with newest joy
my glimmering world entwined upon your word.

Why then am I so bloody afraid?

In Absentia

Scrounging solace from scraps of remembered talk
                  I wander about the bleak November house
                        from room to eyeless room
my mind plucking at fragments
                    at images that would hold it
                      back from the final zero plunge
knowing the absurdity of my misery
                        knowing you will be back
                  but in the small infinities before noon
night is a receding promise.

I search in these vacant hours
                    when flowers are dying
                      for small familiar distractions
in printed word and pictured page
                      in the well-loved antics of our
animals
        and find only a keener melancholy
                  knowing they grieve in your absence too
                    without tongue to put to it.

Scrounging broken scraps of solace
                    from room to heartless room
a disgruntled disinherited ghost
                    I observe the jaded grass
                      below my window
dry and brittle as hope gone sour
                    a lone sparrow talking to itself
                      on a dead branch.

Dark and there will come the swish and glide of wheels
                      on wet gravel
                      doors opening and
shutting

　　　　　　　　your step and voice in the kitchen
　　　　　　　　　　　the dogs frantic in welcome
the more sedate greeting of the cat
　　　　　　　　　　　curling herself round your
insteps.

You will be tired
　　　　　　　　but you will smile and touch my hair
　　　　　　　　　　　and ask me how I spent *my* day
and not being brave I will tell you.

We will laugh and have a few slow drinks by the fire
　　　　　　　　　　and in the night next to you
　　　　　　　　　　　most near as my own lulled flesh
I will be tortured by a dream of you
　　　　　　　　　　　　never coming back.

Visitors

Soft upon a whispered adieu
the moonlit visitors sail out
jewelled with remembrance
upon their bright coffin slabs
out of sight and never out of mind
behind the silver lisp of faint shore voices
burning forever in singing stones

A look spearing folded leaves
fragile brush of fingertips
ineffable and certain as the wind
a dialogue the shuttered brain cannot snare
and a star hisses headlong to earth
trailing immemorial airs
as footfalls die

A cloud stirs upon the moon
a slow sure wink
and fragrant waves below
inform the night with peace

In my room of midnight rhymes
the loud busy chat of the fire
the book spread sacrificial upon the table
I inhabit again the old cosy dimensions
and ponder on the new friends I have made
in all the mute moonlit eloquence of death
telling me this place is mine and theirs

and the shadows will ever be kind to me.

Old Lady

Miss Mahaffey was her name
all faded lace and silver hair
her face already a skull upon the pillow
lit eerily at night from the streetlight
beaming at the mouth of the narrow lane
below the dull distempered walls of her ward

a frail rainbow fall of silk
faintly smudged at the edges
was little Miss Mahaffey
shrunken and sunken into yesterday
fragile shadow on parched landscape
fingers stirring like limp mice
twitching on the winding shrouds of sheets
maiden lady clinging to grace and dignity
gently lying in her perpetual twilight
not bothering the hurrying nurses for a drop of water
brought by life's meaner barbarities to this
wrinkled and shrivelled up in a crisp bed
coughing up phlegm and speckled blood
being incontinent in the night

a genteel ghost whispering words of no complaint
patient as the plot of earth marked out
to receive her few fish-thin bones
all beauty safely behind her
save briefly when she opened her eyes
to the night nurse bending over her
and murmured "sorry".

Harlequinade

Out of the dark
into a place of song
night a concourse of bright tongues
light outwitting the stars
in galaxies of required glamour

Hear behind the talk
rising behind the tinkle of raised glass
a small cry of need
a cry from the maimed
the forgotten and dispossessed
in whose behalf now
this banquet of no charity is laid
and the nightlong dance begins

Contemplate without malice
from a subtle distance without
this rainbow bowl
of festooned fishes
elegant or estranged
in their respective ecstasies
eddying in perplexed parables of pleasure
engaged in a louder charade
than the one below the surface
muted in patient régimes of pain

Long may the harlequinade spin out
if it takes us away from the tumbrel.

*Also by Christy Brown
and available in Minerva Paperbacks*

Down all the Days

The triumphant novel of the slums of Dublin

Pushed around the streets of Dublin by his boisterous brothers, the small crippled occupant of a boxcar is the silent witness of the city's joys and woes. Fully possessed of the thoughts and feelings of his sprawling family, he is the focal figure of the novel which relates his searing childhood and coming of age. At once tormented and relaxed, he is the detached observer of life in the slums of forties and fifties Dublin.

Written with the fearless discipline that Christy Brown had to establish over his own body, *Down all the Days* displays his lyrical gift with language to the full.

'Will surely stand beside Joyce and in front of all the others as Dublin writ large and writ for all times' *Irish Times*

'Deserves the highest critical acclaim, not because it was written with one foot but because it is the work of a real writer who just happens to be handicapped' *Daily Telegraph*

My Left Foot

The warm, humorous and true story of Christy Brown's supreme courage and triumph over the severest of handicaps.

Christy Brown was born a victim of cerebral palsy. But the helpless, lolling baby concealed the brilliantly imaginative and sensitive mind of a writer who would take his place among the giants of Irish literature.

This is Christy Brown's own story. He recounts his childhood struggle to learn to read, write, paint and finally type, with the toe of his left foot. *My Left Foot* is now a major Oscar-winning film starring Daniel Day Lewis as Christy Brown.

'A story of courage that is wise and in no way morbid'
Sunday Times

A Shadow on Summer

The ivory tower of success

The writer of a bestseller, Riley McCombe is anonymous no more. Crippled and publicity-shy, he is catapulted from the slums of Dublin to the wide blue sky of Connecticut and the full blaze of fame. Now he must write another.

While Riley stays with Laurie and Don Emerson, Laurie is only too happy to appoint herself hostess and mentor – and although he resents her criticisms, Riley responds to her warmth and femininity. Then, at one of his American publisher's lavish parties, elegant photographer Abbie Lang chooses to join in the curious tug of war for the young Irishman's love. But Riley, ever fearful of the responsibility of his craft, can only intensify the puzzled hurt of both women while he remains an intensely lonely prisoner of himself.

'Its sharpest insights concern the necessary privateness and privations of creativity'
Valentine Cunningham, *New Statesman*

'Christy Brown's *A Shadow on Summer* . . . maintains the remarkable energy of *Down all the Days*'
Martin Seymour-Smith, *Financial Times*

'It contains many flashes of insight into character and many descriptions of the New England countryside that take one's breath away with their rightness'
Francis King, *Sunday Telegraph*

Wild Grow the Lilies

The laughing drains of Dublin

Fond of the girls at Madame Lala's, eloquent reporter Luke Sheridan is fonder still of the sound of his own voice. Bursting with purple prose and ribald repartee, he even dreams of writing *the* Great Irish Novel.

But work comes first – especially when Dublin's evening newspaper is tipped off about the attempted murder of a German count. Going after the scoop of the year, Luke is helplessly and hilariously mixed up in the most wildly flamboyant goose chase that ever crossed the fair city's underbelly.

'*Wild Grow the Lilies*, lively, fluent and derivative . . . is a grossly entertaining novel' *Times Literary Supplement*

'Christy Brown has an extraordinary gift for vivid language and imagery' *The Times*

'Christy's romp is thoroughly enjoyable . . . It is wildly funny, bawdy and vulgar and the writing, whether sonorous or broad Dublin, is a delight'
Catherine O'Faolain, *Irish Press*

A Promising Career

The fickle world of show biz

Married at seventeen, Art and Janice have more than their love to sustain a partnership – their talent. For both show considerable promise as musicians, as charismatic agent, Simon Sandford, is quick to observe. Under his tutelage, the young couple begin to flourish in the labyrinthine ambit of gigs, tours and recording sessions.

Yet success only seems to accentuate their differences. And Sandford, a seasoned manipulator of this corrupt and exploitative world, has his own wedge to drive . . .

Christy Brown finished *A Promising Career* shortly before his tragic death in 1981. A departure from his astonishing autobiography – and unforgettable film – *My Left Foot*, and also from his native Ireland, it is perhaps his most mature and imaginative novel.

A Selected List of Titles Available from Minerva

While every effort is made to keep prices low, it is sometimes necessary to increase prices at short notice. Mandarin Paperbacks reserves the right to show new retail prices on covers which may differ from those previously advertised in the text or elsewhere.

The prices shown below were correct at the time of going to press.

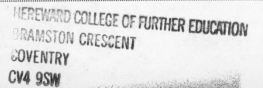